# Self, System and the Non-Conscious:

## The Further Metaphysics of Meaning and Mystery

Laurence Peddle

Copyright © Laurence Peddle
All rights reserved.

Paperback Print ISBN 978-0-9955317-1-0

The right of Laurence Peddle to be identified as the author of this work has been asserted by him in accordance with the Copyright Designs and Patents Act 1988

No part of this publication may be reproduced, stored in a retrieval system, or transmitted in any form or by any means without the prior permission in writing of the publisher. Nor be otherwise circulated in any form or binding or cover other than that in which it is published and without a similar condition being imposed on the subsequent purchaser.

Published by
Llyfrau Cambria Books, Wales, United Kingdom.
*Cambria Books is a division of*
*Cambria Publishing Ltd.*
Discover our other books at: www.cambriabooks.co.uk

# On Newport Bridge 1988

Years later now, an older man it seems
In contrast to the boy with visions lit by hopeful schemes
sated now, misled by blind addiction
but spared at least self-pity for this self-imposed affliction.
I dreamt in colour then but cannot now recall who dreamed,
inspired by the radio and hymn like songs that seemed
to echo long ago those gospel tunes by Motown blades,
with lyrics painting endless love behind those hipster shades.

Western patriarchal gods I prayed to in my youth,
or Eastern koans I meditated on in my careless search for truth,
tabs of acid, grams of speed
or flagons of alcohol and vomit while the needle syphoned love.

I stumbled willingly across the bridge each night,
Over the river Usk, blessing the patterns from the docked boats' light,
every winding backstreet seemed like the blueprint for some plan,
That led me onward to a knowledge of the ways of man.

I walked across that bridge once more tonight,
A squanderer of words and empty years and love's lost light,
Just a wanderer in a 60's suit from some Dock Street Oxfam shop
Wishing with every wasted breath this cold night crossing would stop.

Mike McNamara; taken from his poetry book *Dialling a Starless Past*.

## Death's Echo

The desires of the heart are as crooked as corkscrews
    Not to be born is the best for man.
The second best is a formal order
    The dance's pattern, dance while you can.
Dance, dance, for the figure is easy
    The tune is catching and will not stop
Dance till the stars come down with the rafters
    Dance, dance, dance till you drop.

                          — W.H. Auden

# Preface and Acknowledgements

The origins of this book are of horticultural interest, though only figuratively, concerning as they do the uprooting of several chapters from the first drafts of what would eventually become *The Mystery Beyond Knowledge: Scepticism, Intentionality, and the Non-Conscious*. This deracination, in the strict sense, was forced mainly upon the probability sections, which ran riot over my carefully cultivated plot, the main topics feeling the squeeze, and the mathematics in any case too technical. My aim, after all, was to appeal, or rather for the book to appeal, to any reader making metaphysical enquiries of the world, whereas not even all philosophers, let alone the curious in general, are on speaking terms with the probability calculus.

And yet, I have seen fit to incorporate these tangled plants into this new border of the present work, my excuse for which is that one can always hop and skip through such dense undergrowth, which will trip you out onto wider paths, leading as they do to the easier topics listed in the table of contents. These comprise the probability chapters and the chapter on Molyneux' Problem, itself retrieved from the compost heap, together with a much more detailed chapter on perception. Also, freshly grown chapters on consciousness and on the problems of personal identity, which would certainly have featured in *Beyond Knowledge* had space permitted. Its eminent suitability derives from the aims and methods of that work, which I have summarised in the introduction to this one, thereby enabling its independence and separate existence. The acorn, however, does not fall far from the tree, my intention being to again employ the notion of a system in solving the various problems, for instance to show that probability theory is amenable to that approach.

Speaking of acorns, or icons, this being the acknowledgement section, I again pay tribute to Christopher Norris, who has never wavered in supporting me. It was Christopher who restored my academic self-confidence and constantly reassured me as to the worth of the book I was writing; and similarly with the present work, which he encouraged me to persevere with and to submit for publication. Both books, or volumes if you like, would be the poorer without Christopher's guidance, and in particular they would be less enlivened by the occasional witticism or droll remark, the appropriateness of which I sometimes had my doubts about. He has also been an emotional support and sympathetic listener, the same as Valerie Norris, into whose novels, in addition, I sometimes escape. And, too, I am grateful to my publisher, Chris Jones of Cambria Publishing UK, for all his help, and especially for the impressively speedy transition from acceptance to print; to my partner, Valerie Rogers, for caring for me every day and every hour, despite her partner always having been an obstacle to an easy relationship; and to Carolyn Michel of Design Elements for the book cover. My thanks again to Mike McNamara as poet, and to him as leader of the Big Mac Wholly Soul Band, which has brought so much joy into my life and that of all the band's fans, who are legion.

    I am grateful, also, to the staff at Velindre Hospital for their toxic treatment of metastasising tumours, comparable in its effects only to the collateral chemo damage done to all bodily systems. Finally, I must thank myself for my insightful self-pity; for my silent scream in the skin and bone of the suicidal homicide perpetrated by cancer; and for the impotent rage that I gob in the face of death and dying, which in the abominable end are the final despotism by which men and women, desperate not to die, are humiliated and oppressed.

# CONTENTS

**Introduction**   1
   1: The General Approach   1
   2: The Present Work   4

**Chapter 1: Consciousness Confined**   9
   1.1: The Reality of Other People   11
   1.2: From Conceiving to Empathising   13
   1.3: The Sceptical Arguments   15
   1.4: Privileged Access   21
   1.5: Conclusions   25

**Chapter 2: System and Intentionality**   26
   2.1: Phenomenological Versus Intentional   29
   2.2: The Myth of Conscious Adequacy   32
   2.3: The Non-Conscious Under Fire   34

**Chapter 3: The Problem of Perception**   41
   3.1: Scepticism Confronted   44
   3.2: Are Sense Data Real?   47
   3.3: Primary and Secondary Qualities   51
   3.4: Towards Perceptual Intentionality   53
   3.5: Perception and Conception   59
   3.6: Smith's Proposed Solution   64
   3.7: Judgement Day   65

**Chapter 4: Perceiving the Senses**   68
   4.1: Perceptual Variability   74
   4.2: Illusion as Argument   76
   4.3: Direct Realism   78

| | |
|---|---|
| 4.4: Perception and its Imperatives | 80 |
| **Chapter 5: Probability and its Problems** | **82** |
| 5.1: Types of Probability | 82 |
| 5.2: The Role of Frequency | 87 |
| 5.3: Keynes and Logical Probability | 89 |
| **Chapter 6: The No-Miracles Argument** | **95** |
| 6.1: The Base-Rate Fallacy | 98 |
| 6.2: The NMA and Science | 101 |
| 6.3: Return to the Tea-Tasting Woman | 104 |
| 6.4: Logical Status of the NMA | 108 |
| **Chapter 7: Bayesian Inference** | **111** |
| 7.1: Discrete Distributions | 116 |
| 7.2: Continuous Distributions | 119 |
| 7.3: Maximum Likelihood Estimate | 121 |
| 7.4: The Probability of Success | 123 |
| 7.5: System, Sub-System and Resolution | 126 |
| 7.6: Conclusions | 130 |
| **Chapter 8: Personal Identity** | **132** |
| 8.1: Hume's Empiricist Philosophy | 134 |
| 8.2: Scepticism and Consistency | 136 |
| 8.3: Personal Identity and its Problems | 140 |
| 8.4: Intentionality and the Non-Conscious | 145 |
| 8.5: Avowals and First-Person Identity | 146 |
| 8.6: Surviving the Self | 146 |
| **Chapter 9: The Indeterminate Person** | **150** |
| 9.1: The Unimportance of Identity | 157 |
| 9.2: The Unmaking of Assumptions | 159 |
| 9.3: Recapitulation and a Personal Identity Puzzle | 162 |

| | |
|---|---|
| 9.4: Going Deeper and Drawing Conclusions | 167 |
| 9.5: My Own Personal Identity and Self | 168 |
| 9.6: Death and Mystery | 172 |
| 9.7: Last Words | 173 |
| **Bibliography** | **176** |
| **Endnotes** | **181** |

# Introduction

My aim in this book is to deepen and extend my discussion of some of the philosophical issues addressed in its predecessor: *The Mystery Beyond Knowledge: Scepticism, Intentionality, and the Non-Conscious*. These issues concern the epistemological and conceptual problems attaching to the philosophy of perception, of consciousness, and of probability. The present work will also parade several chapters on the new topic of personal identity, the chapters on consciousness and probability also being for the most part unpublished. With regard to the topics carried over, my intention is to place them upright herein, and in such a way that they stand on their own rather than having to lean on *Beyond Knowledge*, this being my short way with the title of the first book. There is no denying, that said, that a reading of the first volume will enrich one's understanding of the present one, mainly because the former is more comprehensive. Since, however, some of us cannot afford to be enriched, and given my stated intention, my plan for this introduction is to condense the main points and general approach of that volume into a summary that will serve as a preliminary to the present work.

## 1: The General Approach

In *Beyond Knowledge* I present a system-based solution to traditional epistemological and conceptual problems and, on the same basis, a non-empiricist theory of knowledge. It is only by striking out in this new direction, in my opinion, that the issues may be resolved. The system referred to is that by which the concepts of intention, induction, perception, avowals, the past and other minds are interconnected, interdependent and governed by necessary conditions of application.

By way of illustration, suppose that I report that I am looking at this keyboard, the palm rest of which I see as curved, my seeing of it being an occurrent perceptual event. Yet what I see at one moment or from one perspective is evidentially accountable to further such experience. If I move my head a little to the side, I expect the palm rest to continue to look curved and any newly visible part of it to dovetail with the old. Such micro-expectations, as I call them, are necessary to perception, as is perceptual expectation at further remove. If I hold the keyboard at eye level, turning it until it is end-on, then I expect to see the palm rest in curved profile, confirmatory of its previous appearance and of the corresponding perceptual beliefs. A condition here is that I remember that appearance and, since the keyboard is a solid, stable object, that I expect it to persist from one moment to the next, other things being equal, and to be able to re-identify it.

Since the problem of induction connects with perception, Hume's anti-inductive arguments, radically interpreted, gain purchase on perceptual prediction, my claim being that they also challenge one's knowledge of the past. Reasoning in this way, I try to show that radical inductive scepticism – the thesis that nothing justifies predictive belief – threatens the whole of knowledge when taken to its logical extremes, an extension which aligns it with epistemological solipsism. This latter, however, I take to be strictly unbelievable, which is enough to condemn it, and I show that in any case it refutes itself. In presenting his argument, the radical inductive sceptic necessarily implies that he remembers the first part and anticipates the last part of the sentences by which the argument is conveyed. He also implies that he grasps his own meaning, his understanding of which is dispositionally accountable to the conditional future. Thus it is that he refutes himself by implying knowledge of the past and the future in the very act of rejecting it.

Arguing in this way, I try to show, given the refutation of such radical scepticism, that the induction problem must be reinterpreted as concerning not whether but *how* we know, so that the difficulties we face, albeit confusedly, are those of analysis. This, it seems to me, is in some ways the approach we perhaps unwittingly already take, even in the case of inductive scepticism. That is, the validity of empirical knowledge, including the prediction intrinsic to it, is presupposed in the statement of the induction problem and in its attempted solutions. Those that involve probability, for example, take for granted that individual balls, dice, urns and bags are re-identifiable.

The approach I have just illustrated has general application, a concomitant of which is that fact and logic need not be in separate spheres; for the synthetic *a priori* links them within a system. A hollow object of uniform thickness *must* have inner corresponding to outer, for instance concave to convex. Perceptual expectations, a case in point being the keyboard examined earlier, are governed by such imperatives.

My secondary aim is to exhibit system-based solution and explanation as being limited in metaphysical scope, beyond which there are only mysteries. Since these are interconnected, they combine into ultimate mystery, itself associated with the impossibility of escape from the system. Consider the problem of one's knowledge of the past and let the sceptic state his case—basically that such knowledge is ultimately dependent on memory, which cannot be directly confirmed once the remembered event has come and gone. The rejoinder here is that the sceptic necessarily refutes himself in his unavoidable reliance on the memories that enter into the case that he states. Now suppose that the sceptic accepts this anti-sceptical argument and retires from the fray. Then he may well be dissatisfied with that solution, for it does not consist in a proof that one enjoys direct epistemic access to past events. But even if he accepts that no such access is possible, he may still be in thrall to philosophical perplexity, not so much about what we know of the past as about what it is to know it. This, however, lives next door to mystery.

For suppose that I now recollect opening a present on my fifth birthday and that in my mind's eye I see the wrapping paper come off, where in terms of the phenomenological this equates with mental imagery. If at this level the sceptic about intentionality tries to reduce memory to mental event, as if it were a sensation, then it may be shown that he refutes himself and that memory is irreducibly intentional. But the fact remains that remembering a past event is a present conscious process, its intentionality being wholly inscrutable. Since the sceptic's perplexed interrogation of the concept of the past never forces it to reveal its identity, the spotlight should turn to system-based analysis — but we have seen that post-analysis the sceptic remains perplexed.

If that analysis fails to satisfy him, despite his not being able to fault it, and given that there are no longer any problems the solving of which might succeed where analysis fails, the only possibility still standing is that of reinterpreting philosophical perplexity as unquiet awareness of metaphysical mystery. What this means in the present case is that the problem remaining to the erstwhile sceptic, apart from difficulties of analysis, is that of cognitive adjustment, faced as he is with the impenetrable mystery of the irreducibly intentional, for instance in the case of memory and of linguistic meaning.

In the same way it may also be shown that the solution to other problems in terms of a system also reveals mysteries and that they combine. It follows not at all, however, that nothing more can be said, this being the crossroads at which a new theory of intentionality points the way, the intellect in its travels arriving at an altogether novel notion: that of the non-conscious. It reveals itself as the chapters gain momentum, sometimes obscured but always shining brighter when seen, until its full explanatory power is projected back along the road.

## 2: The Present Work

Finally, we need to relate the notion of a system to the subject matter of the present work. The first chapter devotes itself to theory of consciousness, the sceptical approach to which is manifested in epiphenomenalism, the thesis that consciousness lacks the causal efficacy that everyday wisdom credits it with. Favouring the received view, I support it by a Humean analysis of the notion of causation as correlation, thereby re-positioning conscious efficacy on a wider plinth. The second chapter seeks to connect the conscious, the non-conscious and the intentional, my treatment of which is more wide-ranging than in the first book.

The next chapters concern perception, about which my aim in *Beyond Knowledge* was to show that variability of appearance is intrinsic to perceptual processes and does not lend itself to scepticism, for instance in the form of the argument from illusion. Visual appearance varies three-dimensionally according to perspective, distance, illumination and ocular conditions, all of which is compatible with direct realism. Furthermore, perception is intentional and in particular it is inferential, as already shown in the case of the keyboard. Changing the example, when I look at this bottle on the table in front of me it has a certain appearance, which alters very slightly when I shift my chair a little to the right, the new appearance being one that I expect to jigsaw with the old, which I therefore have to remember; but also to expect again if I now return my chair to its original position.

In the present work I extend the discussion and present a detailed critique of A.D. Smith's *The Problem of Perception*. It features a thoroughgoing account of the arguments of the perceptual sceptic, together with Smith's proposed solution to the sceptical problem.

If we now turn to the chapters on probability, my aim in *Beyond Knowledge* was twofold: first, to show that probability theory partakes of both logic and fact, for instance in the matter of relative frequency, which in my view is a probability concept and therefore not wholly empirical. Second, and not so easy to pin down, to show that the theory is governed by necessary conditions, for instance insofar as it concerns the notion of equiprobability, these being such as to permit the application of the theory to the world. This has implications for a common criticism of the Bayesian practice of positing equal priors, namely that their being equal has frequency truth conditions, which the Bayesian may not know to be satisfied.

No doubt this is true, I say in the earlier work, but only in certain circumstances; for it is also true that verifying that the truth conditions obtain is itself a process in which a set of possibilities are treated as being equal. Recall, in this connection, the remark just made about frequency in a probability context being itself a probability concept. If I am told that each of two balls in a bag is either black or red, I may insist, as against the Bayesians and, indeed, those who subscribe to logical probability theory, that I know nothing of the probability of a ball of a particular colour being drawn. It is true that if the balls are equally likely to be drawn, then the probability of red, say, is either 1, $\frac{1}{2}$ or 0, but I do not know that they are equiprobable in that way.

That, at least, is the sceptical stance it is possible to take, for instance if the sceptic is an empiricist. Set against this, however, is the fact that a series of trials would result in a sequence of reds and blacks, and it would have to be subjected to statistical tests if the actual probabilities were to be ascertained, this being the sense in which relative frequency is a probability construct. For a frequency estimate to be based on the outcomes of a number of trials they would have to satisfy the requirements of independence and randomness; and, too, assumptions of equiprobability would have to be made. It is within probability theory itself that the notion of equiprobability acquires content

Another way in which probability theory is amenable to system-based analysis is via the notion of underdetermination. Such theory, after all, concerns the inference from sample to population or proportion, these latter extending over a range of possible constitutions that any particular sample is compatible with. Conversely, any particular population or proportion is compatible with a range of samples. How must the two sets be related if the theory is to have application? The answer is that they feed into each other within a system.

Consider a simple rule by which inference from a sample may proceed: that of scaling up. If a bag contains a hundred balls, of which ten are drawn and replaced, with nine found to be black and one white, then the rule is to extrapolate to ninety black balls and ten white balls as the colour content of the balls in the bag. But now, the sample is compatible with any colour proportion apart from all the balls being white, or all black, for instance ninety-nine white and one black. There is nothing in the sample itself to suggest any particular proportion or upper or lower limits if a range is considered.

That problem is resolved if the notion of a system or sub-system is brought to bear, thereby revealing that the probability sub-system is closed in certain ways, for instance with respect to confirmation in the general case. The idea is to consider not a single trial but scaling up as a general method that is validated in terms of frequency. That is, we conduct an experiment in which for numerous trials ten balls are drawn with replacement from a bag containing a hundred black or white balls, the sample colour proportion then being scaled up to give the estimated colour proportion of the balls. It may then be shown that the frequency of a close match between estimate and actual colour proportion is greater than it would be if that proportion was arrived at by random guesswork. This validates the method, the point being that frequency, as already argued for, is a probability construct, this being the sense in which the sub-system is closed, just as it is in the case of equiprobability.

Finally, there are numerous links between the sub-system and more extended system, for instance with regard to underdetermination. My contention is that underdetermination, far from being the sceptic's friend, is a necessary condition of knowing anything at all, both in probability theory and in the case of reasoning in general about the world. Again, frequency is a probability construct in the sub-system but with close connections to everyday use. If, for instance, the ten balls in the sample are given by $(b_9 w_1)$, then calculation is not needed, other things being equal, if our only concern is to decide which colour—namely black— is the more likely to be drawn.

Why do other things need to be equal? What is needed is to assume that the balls, even if only very roughly, are equally likely to be drawn; otherwise we can have no expectation as to colour. Generalising, we could have no expectation as to anything at all, since all expectation is underdetermined.

Let us now turn to the completely new topic—that of personal identity and its problems. Starting from scratch, and with my own identity in an advisory capacity, I soon began to appreciate the difficulties attending the central problem: that of what it is that personal identity consists in. Their severity corresponds to the extremism of some of the proposed solutions, in particular the stance taken by Derek Parfit, who contends that if, in the interests of research, I donate a brain hemisphere, taken to have all the functionality of the intact brain, to an otherwise healthy brainless patient, then it is unimportant if I die. This follows from what Parfit calls the brain-based psychological criterion, whereby the brain is the seat of consciousness, not the body.

Since the beneficiary of my largesse now has half my brain, he qualifies as me according to the criterion. Therefore, I shall survive death. It would be much more reasonable, one might think, to reject the criterion, but retaining it is, I suppose, more fun, and in any case it is of the nature of science fantasy, not fact. My own solution is, as one would expect, system-based, the inner core of personal identity being found in the non-conscious realm, its nature unknowable.

Finally, I end the present work by closing the circle of the two books. This is accomplished by returning to the young couple who featured in the last paragraph of *Beyond Knowledge*, where we left them in the pool in the hills above my childhood home. Our reflections were once on the water, as were the footprints made by our bare feet; but the stream carried them away; and even the water is different now, and always the same. And the young couple we fell in with in the pool—they, too, are different but always the same. Either that or we die another death every day, our former selves lifeless under layers of time elapsed.

# Chapter 1: Consciousness Confined

What I propose is to tease out the connections between the intentional, the conscious and the notion of a system, thereby illuminating by analysis their essential properties. It should also be possible to resolve some of the associated issues, the sceptic being spoilt for choice in this arena, which features disputes about aetiology and causal efficacy. Can one conscious event cause another, as with hearing a loud roaring noise and feeling fear? Can it impact upon the physical, the fear causing a fight or flight or freeze reaction? These questions would seem to be their own affirmative answers, but the sceptic would disagree, his concern being with epiphenomenalism. At the end of this chapter it will be ours, too, but we shall begin with the conceptual problems of other minds.

The everyday view about concepts of consciousness is that mental predicates are univocal irrespective of person, so that "pain", for instance, means the same whether I say that I am in pain or that you are. This assumption of semantic identity is rejected by the radical conceptual sceptic, his basic argument running as follows: since the mental states I experience are necessarily mine, I cannot acquire the concept of a subject of consciousness other than myself.

In examining this argument, we require the sceptic to give some account of his interactions with other people and his apparently attributing consciousness to them, and the only theory setting sail, as far as I can see, is that of behaviourism. With regard to physicalism, for example, it concerns neural-mental identity rather than conceptual constraint; and functionalism as usually understood loosens the nexus between inner consciousness and outward behaviour but does not seek to equate them. If we take it that radical conceptual scepticism entails behaviourism, then we need to ask whether the waves created by the sceptical thesis are so disruptive of our system of interpersonal beliefs, thereby being strictly incredible, that any supporting arguments will always be washed overboard.

The reason for such disruption is that the theory of behaviourism is much more destructive of one's conceptual scheme than it may seem on first acquaintance. The picture one may have is of each individual being conscious at the same time as his ascription of mental states to other people reduces to the associated behaviour. But this is a contradiction; for it is only when I, the present author, self-ascribe mental states that the ascription is not reductive. The self-ascription of consciousness on the part of other people is behaviouristic, which is to say that it reduces to verbal utterances, just as it would with machines that have the power of speech; which, indeed, is precisely what other people are as a consequence of the theory. Since it would follow that I am the only conscious being, reductive behaviourism equates with psychological solipsism; but this latter theory is beyond rational belief.

The fact is, after all, that philosophers bring to the issue a distinction which they, in common with everyone else, entirely take for granted, so that in that sense they are convinced that it holds. They distinguish, that is, between inner mental state and outward behaviour, a distinction they apply both to themselves and to others. Since they are not going to sacrifice it on the altar of radical scepticism unless there are compelling reasons, it is for the sceptic to supply them if he wishes to gain converts.

How can I be sure, that said, that people are unanimous in their rejection of psychological solipsism? Perhaps there are solipsists who are convinced that it is impossible to conceive of other minds, and yet they cannot help believing that they do conceive of them. It is in a similar way that Hume is taken by some commentators to radically reject in theory the scheme of reasoning by which in practice he survived from one day to the next, for instance by electing to exit his house via the stairs as opposed to the window. Nevertheless, it is not as if the sceptic is admitting to a particular belief or set of beliefs that he recognises as being irrational at the same time as he is unable to divest himself of them — or, in Hume's case, to defenestrate himself.

If such recognition obtains, then the sceptics are remarkably adept at dissembling on this point, for they give not the slightest hint of struggling manfully with irrational belief, neither in their interactions nor, indeed, in their philosophising. Believing that one conceives of other minds is not a form of conceptual arachnophobia, as if we are caught in a web of irrational thought; rather, it permeates the whole network of beliefs, concepts, predictions and explanations, conditions and connections by which we observe and interact with other people and with ourselves.

## 1.1: The Reality of Other People

I shall now try to render as vividly as I humanly can the reality of other minds, so that we may realise how much is at stake when the sceptic denies that he can conceive of others' mental states. Suppose, assuming a moratorium on scepticism in the present section, that another person and myself are looking at a uniformly blue wall, and that the similarity between our colour experiences is as great as possible. Then it is my contention that they may be exactly the same, and in the same way as my own such experiences, so that they are qualitatively identical. To bring out the essence of what this means, let us consider objections to it, one of which concerns personal identity. The argument, or perhaps unwitting assumption, is that even if my perceptual experience is the same as the other person's, what this could mean is constrained by the fact that we have separate identities, so that for each of us our unique self runs through our own experiences like a name through a stick of rock. To this the reply may be, following Hume, that I am not acquainted with myself as a subject of whom experiences are predicated, for the self is not an introspectible object.

One could argue, too, that even if it *were* such an object, the experience of it could be both the same for all of us and distinguishable from other kinds of experience, for instance that of blue. There is, of course, the grammatical subject, as when one says 'I am immersed in blueness', but again this reference to oneself may be exactly the same phenomenally as the other person's. That leaves dispositional differences, but there is no reason why these, too, should not be similar. Again, then, we are back with my experience of blue being qualitatively identical with the other person's. It follows that the felt reality of that experience may be *the same for both of us*. That, at least, would be the everyday view if the light of philosophical reflection was projected upon it.

This is a startling result, and it does need to be emphasised, one reason for which is that in everyday life we are all pragmatic behaviourists up to a point — or, better, we are functionalists in our ordinary transactions with other people. That is, we may care very little what experience another person has, for instance when serving us at a counter, the practical emphasis being on the associated behaviour and action. Again, If a passenger in a car knows that the driver is colour blind, her concern is with whether he stops at red and starts again at green, just as it would be if she herself as a driver was afflicted in the same way; and in both cases she need not know exactly what the visual difference consists in or would consist in. This may be generalised, and there is much more that could be said; but it will always fall short of the actual philosophical theory of functionalism, if only for the reason that if I observe a person exhibiting pain behaviour, and if everything points to her being in pain, perhaps because the driver did not, after all, stop at red, then that is what I believe: that she is in pain.

The point is that I may not know exactly what she is feeling, or remember exactly what I felt after my own traffic accident at some time in the past, but I can conceive of her present and my past pain being exactly the same, just as I can of any future pain of mine being exactly the same. And what applies to sensations also applies to colours. That mentalistically we have so much in common with others is, to repeat, an astonishing fact; and what it shows is that there is not just a gap but a chasm between premiss and conclusion when I infer to another's particular conscious state; for its existence is not demonstrable, the same being true of the blanket belief that consciousness resides in this other person.

Now note the following: that none of this is to imply, if the previous paragraph serves as a corrective to the one before, that when we are interacting not with a shopkeeper but with a relative, spouse or close friend, we reach out to them in the shared solidarity of similarity of conscious mental state. All that is in question is the scope and limits of conceivability in the present context, not the possibility of communion with other people on the basis of their being like us. Some people, if anthropo-morphism is not for them, prefer dogs to humans, not because they are like us but because they are not.

Moving on, we need to keep in mind that the notion of conceivability is as vague as it is obscure—all the more so if I can judge whether a thing is conceivable simply by reflecting on it rather than engaging with it. Quite often, that said, there is very little to engage with, for instance if I ask myself whether I can conceive of an individual seeing a blue wall when he looks at it. In seeking an answer, I would have little to gain from observing such an individual, even if I asked him to describe what he saw. His answer, that he saw blue, would at least rule out his being colour blind, other things being equal, but that is all.

If I now switch to imagining that individual as myself, I do not anticipate any grinding of gears or powering up of machinery or automatic re-tooling as a change is made from conceiving of others' experience of blue to conceiving of my own. All that we are discussing, after all, is conceivability, and it seems to me that psychological solipsism is itself conceivable. Indeed, I believe that it is possible to be a genuine psychological solipsist, which is to say an individual who is unable to conceive of humanoid objects as being conscious, this being associated with a failure to see them as behaving similarly to himself.

## 1.2: From Conceiving to Empathising

Perhaps we should now consider the difference between conceiving of a mental state and knowing what it is like to experience it. Based on his knowledge of chiropterology, Thomas Nagel asked what it is like for a bat to be a bat when it deploys its echo-location sense, his point being that the answer lies outside our cognitive purview. Since this is an extreme case, it is worth asking whether we are similarly restricted closer to home. Do we know what it is like for a cat to be a cat?

If we feel that we do not know, this is partly because, as with conceivability, the notion under review suffers from vagueness. And yet, we may also feel that there are genuine cognitive limitations in play, and even that one person's understanding of another is thereby circumscribed. This is the opposite extreme, given the psychological commonality by which human beings are interchangeable; but I think that a case can be made for the existence of cognitive barriers, even between one person and another.

If, to begin with, we feel cognitively excluded when we see dogs playing together, or when our pet dog is gazing inscrutably at us, then we are also on the outside looking in when the dogs are replaced by chimpanzees. But if our closest biological relatives, then why not babies or toddlers? And if we do not know what it is to be a child, then surely that feeling of cognitive alienation extends to what it is like to be a teenager—and so on until all ages are beyond our purview. If this is correct, then it would seem that Nagel misled himself when he targeted inter-specific differences; though another possibility is that I have misconstrued what he meant.

There is, as it happens, a way of putting this to the test, the first step being to recruit into an experiment the person, perhaps one's wife, whom we may feel that we know better than anyone else. Now sit the subject down, this being a formal experiment, and give her a newspaper to read so that we can observe her without any distracting interacting. Our objective is to identify with her in the sense of knowing what it is like for her when she is reading a text. Given the vagueness already referred to, the best I can do, by way of assisting the experiment, is to delineate ostensively the cognitive inability in question by pointing to the way in which it manifests itself in the present case.

Such inability has nothing to do with the wealth of information about her that one may have accrued throughout one's married life if one is at all observant. The inability we are seeking to discover in ourselves is marked by poverty, not wealth, and it consists in our struggling, to no avail, to identify with her so completely that we share with her not the experience of reading, as if we had our own copy of the newspaper, but *her* experience of reading. We will always fail, of course, in the light of which it is quite likely that we cease to make the attempt and simply note that we cannot know what it is for her to be her.

The above analysis is elucidatory, insofar as that is possible, of a notion that is both disjointed and profound. I have attempted to bring it into relief, a process that the following further analysis will take as far as it can go. I said just now that our need to share the subject's reading experience cannot be met by our reading a copy of the same article, otherwise there would be no difficulty. And yet, it may seem to us in our cognitive turmoil that we should be able, given our own reading experience, to know what it is like for her when she reads a text.

Similarly, given one's own experience of physical pain, one may feel that it should be possible to know what it is for another person to suffer in the same way, even if it is not at all clear how the similar experiences are cognitively connected. That such a connection exists would seem to be a widespread assumption, as the forthcoming discussion of ascribing mental states to ourselves and others will attest. The present finding is that one may distinguish between conceiving of others as being conscious and knowing what consciousness is like for them, or for them to have a particular conscious experience.

## 1.3: The Sceptical Arguments

In his contribution to a journal article on the conceptual problem of other minds, Colin McGinn (1984) relates it, via some remarks of Wittgenstein's, to what is known as Molyneux' Question, which runs as follows. Suppose that a congenitally blind person acquaints herself by touch with objects having a square cross-section, so that she thereby acquires the concept, or at least the tactual concept, of squareness. As the "at least" implies, the question is just that of whether the woman, if newly sighted, would immediately be able to recognise square objects without having to touch them first, thereby indicating that she had possessed that ability or disposition, albeit unrealised, when she was blind. According to McGinn, the analogy here is with the question of whether the concept of another's pain, for instance, can be derived from that of one's own pain. We shall ask later whether this analogy is apt.

Our concern is with whether the concept of a particular mental state, or the acquiring of it, is necessarily linked to one's experience of it. Such a link, if it obtains, lends itself to psychological solipsism—the sceptical view that we cannot conceive of other people as being conscious. This brings to mind Nagel's thesis, which I had reservations about, it being enough for the moment to note that the proposition is obscure as it stands, inviting as it does a number of questions. How close, for instance, must the connection be? Do I need to have had toothache in order to grasp the concept of it? Suppose that the sceptic concedes that I do not and grants that past experience of a headache may be a suitable substitute, provided that it throbbed in a similar way to a toothache.

But in what way might that be, and how is one to form a judgement on the matter? Not only that, but if this is a prerequisite then by what criterion is felt pain location exempted? Perhaps we should include it, in which case the concept-forming desiderata are as follows: one is able to grasp the concept of toothache if one has had a toothache-like throbbing pain phenomenally located in one's tooth — in other words if one has had toothache. We shall pass over the question of whether one's previous toothache would qualify only if the affected tooth was the same as the one at the centre of one's present pain. On second thoughts, let us not pass over it, for by what metaphysical intui-tion do we dismiss it, whereas a similar question about felt location is taken more seriously? But this is to imply that very little hangs on it.

To show just how little that is, imagine this time that I have just eaten chocolate as a treat for my oral bacteria and that I now anticipate the onset of toothache, perhaps because of my experience of dental caries and perverse bacterial ingratitude. But if there is a necessary connection between previous pain experience and my grasp of the concept of toothache, then the claim is not that they are logically connected, presumably by way of being analytic. This would be the claim if, for instance, the contention was that one cannot have the concept of toothache if one does not have the concept of pain. What this trades on is the fact that toothache is a form of pain; and whether the contention is correct, if one can be bothered to ask, will depend, uninterest-ingly, on this and that.

The actual claim, however, is that the necessary connection is not between concepts but between the experience of pain and the concept of toothache; and the crucial point is that it would have to be contingent. For if my previous experience of toothache, headache or pain in general effects a concept-acquiring change, which we may suppose to be cerebral in character, whereby I now have the concept of toothache, then it is conceivable that the resulting brain state obtain even in the absence of any history of physical suffering, this also being true of the prediction of toothache that I make. There is, after all, nothing in the conscious phenomena of my understanding of toothache to suggest that previous pain of any kind is non-contingently — or even contingently in a different sense of "necessary" — a necessary condition of my grasp of the concept. It is true that we understand if suitably disposed, but here again there is no contradiction in supposing that the appropriate dispositions are in place.

Note, too, that naturalistically a similar point can be made. That is, it is arguable that in everyday reasoning we make unwarranted assumptions about the closeness of the relation between understanding and experiencing particular kinds of mental state. One example would be that of what it feels like to give birth, which we are said to appreciate only if we ourselves have had babies, it not being an acceptable surrogate that mothers, however articulate, should describe their experiences to us. That leaves witnessing the event at first hand, preferably while the mother-to-be gives a running commentary on her feelings and sensations — but this, too, would perhaps be regarded as failing to deliver the unique insight that only experiencing childbirth for oneself can bring into the world. Interestingly, I did experience childbirth for myself at one time, though in my case it was more like babybirth, but I would not say that it gave me any special insight into the feelings and sensations one has while being born.

Let us now ask whether the same reasoning holds for the cognitive circumstances of the blind woman. It is a contingent fact, if it is a fact at all, that newly sighted she will have to learn to associate the visual and the tactual, thereby revealing this limitation on her previous grasp of shape concepts. But it is easy to imagine otherwise, for instance that upon opening her eyes for the first time she immediately recognises and identifies objects familiar to her from touch, including square tables, round walking sticks and her husband. Moreover, I am about to argue that the two scenarios are not mutually exclusive. If this is correct, as also the claim about contingency, then why exactly is the Molyneux problem thought to be of interest to philosophers? To make the question clear, suppose that the woman is recovering from a successful eye operation, the dressing having just been removed, and that she knows that the person sitting in the chair next to her bed is her husband, having recognised him by his voice. He points at the object he is holding and tells her that she has made daily use of it for years, hence his dis-appointment at her failure to recognise it.

'A failure easily rectified', she thinks, whereupon she grasps the object and immediately recognises it as her white walking stick. 'So this is what white looks like', she exclaims. Running her hand along the stick, knowing in advance that it will feel the same for the whole of its length until the tip is reached, she thereby associates that feeling with visual straightness. Arriving at the tip, she visually identifies the ferrule before touching it, because it looks different from the body of the stick. Should we say, then, that the answer to Molyneux's questions with regard to the ferrule is that she can identify it by sight alone, whereas the stick itself had first to be felt?

Clearly, we can say it if we like, but we may also suppose that the woman handles the ferrule first, thereby associating the look of it with the feel of it, and that she then recognises the body of the stick by sight alone — or, there again, that she immediately recognises both. The important point, as always, is that perception and observation belong within a system, the present case being such that the newly sighted woman immediately engages in a process of incorporating the deliverances of a newly acquired sense into the dynamics of her system of perceptual knowledge.

Why, to return to it, is Molyneux' Question thought to be of philosophical interest? Because the answer will indicate whether the woman had visual identificatory ability when she was blind, this being a necessary condition of her concepts of physical shape being visual as well as non-visual. If, as common sense would suggest, there is indeed such a condition, then the conceptual sceptic would have to maintain, in allowing for the possibility that the condition is fulfilled, that it is necessary but not sufficient; for his thesis, after all, is that the blind woman's grasp of the concept of physical shape is purely tactual. But what, in that case, would the sceptic grant as a sufficient condition? The answer cannot be given in terms of brain states or dispositions, which contingently might obtain, whereas the sceptic's thesis is meant to go deeper; hence my reference to metaphysical truth. His claim is that the woman's experience of the physical world is purely tactual; therefore, on that account alone, the same must be true of her conception of that world, this being a non-contingent conclusion that is metaphysical in character. The appeal, it might be said, is to our deepest empiricist intuitions.

To appeal to empiricism or conceptual foundationalism is not, however, to terminate the discussion, as if it were the last port of call. Indeed, I now propose to lead the sceptic into deeper waters, this time dropping anchor above what appears to be the abyss which separates the phenomenal and the intentional. This latter, or so I have argued, is irreducible within a system. The fact is, after all, that the blind woman's conception of squareness is of square-shaped objects in a physical world which exists independently of being perceived. This transforms the problem, for the three-dimensional world inhabited by the blind woman is the same as that of sighted people, the difference being that the woman cannot see it or any of its occupants. That, at least, is what my deepest intuition tells me.

If we now return to the question of the blind woman's conception of a world visually perceived, then our conclusion is that the different senses available to her reveal the same physical objects as those that are seen. This is truistic at one level, for clearly the woman is able to feel her stick when she touches it, to hear it when she taps it and to see it and recognise it after the operation, either immediately or very shortly after other senses have been brought into play. If it turns out that this latter is needed, so that before the operation she was not disposed to recognise any objects by sight alone, then strictly speaking she did not possess visual concepts. This, I suggest, is of no great import, the point being that they are easily accommodated, a place already marked out for them, in the system of empirical knowledge and observation by which her existing senses are co-ordinated and function separately or in concert. They are intentional in character and inform her of the presence of an independently existing physical world.

If this is correct, then the issue goes far beyond what should, strictly speaking, be said, and, rightly or wrongly, it is metaphysical in the arguments deployed. It concerns the relation, in terms of necessary and contingent, between the concept and the experience of particular mental states; and noteworthy here is that irrespective of the sense modality involved, very little that is at all specific can be said, this being in itself a significant fact. That is, if initially I posit a close connection between concept and experience, then I still have to acknowledge that it is not so close that, for instance, I understand toothache, or what it is like to feel it, only if I have actually felt it myself.

There is a sense of "understand" such that one knows what it is like to have toothache only if one has had it, the same being true of labour pains, with half the human race thereby being cognitively excluded. These combine into an even more exclusive club, the members of which enjoy that esoteric insight vouchsafed only to those who have given birth in a dentist's chair. This is, it seems to me, a very confused and obfuscatory use of the concept of understanding, which perhaps we should eschew not only in philosophy but also in everyday conversation, where it lends itself, in this latter case, to a particularly irritating form of life-event snobbery.

We are now able to return to the original question re-interpreted: not whether one can other-ascribe consciousness but how it is that certain difficulties of conceptual analysis attending that ascription may be resolved. And the answer is implicit in the arguments already presented. The question, it may be recalled, was phrased as follows: how can one derive the concept of another's pain from one's own pain experience? But this is to presuppose that the relation at issue is that of derivation, and it is this implied metaphysical thesis that I have attempted to overturn. If my own pain or ability to feel it is not a necessary condition of my grasp of the concept of pain, which I may possess even if I am not able to feel pain, then the question of how I can ascribe pain to other people on the basis of my own must lapse. This terminates the voyage of the conceptual sceptic about other minds, who now finds himself utterly capsized and all at sea. What remains is to steer a course towards a more metaphysical account of consciousness concepts and their terms and conditions, the place to start being with self-knowledge and the question of its epistemic status.

## 1.4: Privileged Access

To begin with, we should interrogate an assumption that many commentators share with the sceptic; namely, that one is directly acquainted only with one's own consciousness and its particulars. This explains, according to McGinn, why it is that there are difficulties about our conceiving of other people as being similarly blessed. We are broadening our remit to include the epistemological as well as the conceptual, and on the basis of their close connections. It is clear that one is justifiably certain about the wider contents of one's consciousness when compared with one's limited knowledge of the furniture of another person's mind. Looking at one's spouse when she engages in some activity, say reading a newspaper, one has no idea what she may be thinking as she reads, not even if one is reading the same article while studying her.

In general, indeed, we are completely ignorant of the minutiae of the stream of consciousness in another person's inner landscape, knowing only, in the present case, that the subject is reading, the same as we are. But now, we are also ignorant of the details of our own stream of consciousness, for the conscious flow will always overrun any description, no matter how furiously fast we cross and dot it, just as it would with an actual stream. To make the attempt would be like placing a bucket in the water in order to capture the stream at a particular moment, the bucket filling but the stream flowing on.

So far, then, we have not claimed any epistemic privileges, but will that equality continue to hold if we now compare self-ascribed and other-ascribed sensation, the stock example being that of pain? Suppose that in the present case the subject's reading is interrupted when she appears to be stung by a bee, with myself also falling victim to the same or a different assailant. at which point we both yelp, having spent far too much time with dogs. Since I was directly aware of my own pain but aware of hers by way of inference, there would seem to be a difference of degree of certainty. As against this, there are three points to be made.

The first is that either her pain was genuine or it was counterfeited. If I favour the latter, but have no reason apart from the fact of inference, then my suspicions are incoherent, the attempted avoidance of which would entail my having to distrust all empirical knowledge. But this would undermine the position of epistemic privilege by which her claim to having been stung was found wanting in the first place. The reason, familiar to readers of *Beyond Knowledge*, is that the attack has come and gone and the pain with it, so that I now have to trust to my memory of events, than which no knowledge is more indirect, my privileged status thereby being revoked.

Secondly, and following on, is it really a privilege if inspection reveals only a momentary pain? No, you will say, but why should it be momentary? Because even if a sensation is long-lasting we feel it from one moment to the next, each previous moment of it having ceased to exist, the impression of duration owing much to memory and expectation.

Thirdly, I can doubt whether she felt pain only if armed with an explanation of her seeming to feel it, given that I noticed the bee on her arm and can see the stinger it left behind. Perhaps I happen to know that she cannot feel pain but pretends that she can. The original assumption, however, was that my doubts are based entirely on the fact of having to infer to her pain.

Am I suggesting that knowledge of oneself and that of others have equal epistemic status? Not at all, for there are a myriad ways in which I know more about myself than others know about me. That said, it is also true that in some ways others are better placed to pronounce upon my motives in conducting myself in one way rather than another, and upon my character and personality, my abilities, and so on. The deliverances of memory can also go either way, in some cases with other people having a more accurate recall of shared experiences or observations than I do. One could go on, with one case after another being cited either for or against the idea of epistemic privilege.

The fact remains, however, that on the whole I am favourably positioned with regard to knowledge of myself, even in the case of stream of consciousness. My earlier contention was only that the stream cannot be brought under the discipline of description beyond a certain level of detail— that at which a snapshot showing every little surge and ripple at any particular moment is descriptively displayed. But this does not preclude my saying that the stream at a given place and time surged over protruding stones and rippled at the edges. The parallel would be with, for instance, my avowal that I am thinking about philosophy, or epistemology, or self-knowledge, or the fact that much of my stream of consciousness can be known to others only if I bundle it up into the general terms by which I describe it, rather than that I try to create a snapshot.

The essential point, if the connection with acquiring the concept of consciousness is to be secured, is that my privileged access depends upon memory and expectation, the scheme of things being such as to involve necessary conditions. Particular memories may be confirmed or disconfirmed by way of the associated expectations, a process which itself recruits other memories and expectations to the cause. These latter cannot themselves be checked, or not without an infinite regress opening up, the necessary condition being that they go by default. If in the case of a particular memory one asks for its credentials, the authority by which the demand is made must not be such as to extend to all memories, this again being a necessary condition.

If I just have a particular memory with no obvious way to check it, as very frequently happens, then it cannot be doubted for that reason, for all memories are ultimately unsupported, hence yet another necessary condition. One could go on, for instance by showing that memory is actually a belief about a past event, in other words a belief, there being no logical relation between a memory and the event remembered. Much of this analysis, suitably re-phrased, would also apply to avowals, but we have done enough to be able to make the requisite connections.

We concluded that very little of significance at or near the level of metaphysics can be said, and certainly not enough to support the radical scepticism we characterised as a form of psychological solipsism. That the only conscious human being is oneself is a proposition that very few people, the irony noted, genuinely embrace. If they do, then perhaps it is because they cannot bring themselves to hold close, the aversion being reciprocated, what would normally be described as fellow human beings, including their spouses. This would help to explain, as pointed out in *Beyond Knowledge*, why it is that evolutionary processes have not favoured the solipsist. In particular it accounts for the fact that the male psychological solipsist invariably marries into a polyandrous arrangement, a monogamous relationship being out of the question for his wife, given his radically anti-social conceptual scheme.

That the solipsist is in error should be obvious in any case from one's everyday conceptual practice. For instance, my ability to identify my painful sensations, as with the sight-restored woman's ability to make visual identifications, is just one trick in the bag of tricks by which the concept of pain is manifested. Even when I am in pain and thus describe it in the present tense, the hidden reference is to moment by moment past pain, and the transition to the actual use of the past tense, as when I say 'The pain has abated', runs very smoothly indeed. And the same, this being significant, if a person suffering, so to speak, from con-genital analgesia—the inability to feel pain—says 'I have been unable since birth to feel pain.' So it is that the thesis of psychological solipsism collapses.

Finally, we note again that the concepts of memory and expectation, which *are* of metaphysical interest, are intentional, as is the semantic content of the ascription of mental states to ourselves and others. The engine of their phenomenology is therefore located in the non-conscious, which by its very nature is a place of concealment. This illuminates further the mistake that the sceptic makes when he maps the concept of conscious phenomena onto one's experience of them, the link between concept and experience purporting to be both metaphysical and causal. I have argued that any such link belongs to psychology, not philosophy, and certainly not metaphysics.

## 1.5: Conclusions

If the foregoing account is correct, then the conceptual sceptic credits herself with metaphysical access to fundamental laws governing the acquisition of psychological concepts. I have tried to show that the positing of a necessary connection between experience and concept acquisition is out of bounds. This is not to deny that there are metaphysical constraints, just as there are necessary conditions; and both of these are fundamental. But they and our understanding of them obtain within a system—and intrinsic to the notion of a system is that of epistemic limitation of metaphysical scope, beyond which there is only mystery. Here, if anywhere, one's inability to answer the sceptic may momentarily chill into loneliness, as if a window suddenly opens onto winter and is hastily slammed shut. But other people should be inside with us, not out in the cold, the exception being the conceptual sceptic about other minds.

# Chapter 2: System and Intentionality

The notion of a system, as I understand it, transcends the distinction between fact and logic or, in political terms, between the North and South Korea of empiricism and rationalism, with little in the way of diplomacy between them. I wish to show that there exists a middle ground by which they are linked by trade and commerce, to which end I shall now tease out the connections, using transcendental argument, between memory and prediction. The distinction between empiricist and rationalist will then be exposed as being factitious.

Suppose that a sceptic claims to reject memory but not prediction. If he sees an object, say a desktop monitor, and closes his eyes, then he expects to see it when he opens them a moment later but rejects what may seem to him to be his memory of seeing it a moment ago. This, however, is disjointed, for he cannot claim to expect to see a monitor if he lacks moment-by-moment memory of the expectation. But also, an expectation can be confirmed only if memory is involved, without which it cannot qualify as an expectation.

Conversely, it may be shown that he is disqualified from any memory claim if he rejects all knowledge of, in the present case, the immediate future. What we are asked to imagine is that he closes his eyes, remembers looking at the monitor and is about to open them again, all without permitting himself to have any idea of what he can expect to see. When he opens his eyes and sees the monitor, does this at least confirm his memory of having seen it a few moments ago? But there cannot be confirmation, including of memory, without expectation, and for several reasons.

The first, in relation to the memory of perceiving a physical object, in the present case a monitor, is that memory entails recognition or identification. If I say 'I saw a monitor', my implied description is of a three-dimensional object, which is to say that it is accountable to further observation, parts of the monitor being hidden from view. I thereby commit myself to a conditional prediction: that I know what to expect to see from different perspectives relative to the object, by virtue of which I recognise it as a monitor. More particularly, I imply that it persists through time, so that again a prediction is involved. More generally, nothing could count as memory if there were no possibility of confirmation, and nothing could count as confirmation if the future was completely unknowable.

Let us assume that I have made a convincing case for memory and prediction being interdependent, in line with the notion of a system of connections and necessary conditions. What becomes of the empiricist/rationalist distinction and the apparent lack of common ground between them? Prediction and memory are epistemically empirical insofar as mistakes can be made, as indeed they often are, and the errors individually are not logical but factual. But memory and prediction or expectation are interdependent, this being true *a priori*, and the relations between them fall naturally into neither camp, this being the sense in which fact and logic need not be adversaries.

If to this it is objected that what seems to be true of micro-analysis is belied by macro-analysis, then where and how does one draw the line? Note that I am not implying that distinctions in general have to be clearcut—or if I am then some form of brain damage would seem to be indicated. My claim, rather, is that the line in question is arbitrarily drawn; or, better, that in any case micro-analysis will prevail; for macro-analysis depends on it. The fact is, after all, that the observations we make, whatever their duration, are framed by micro-inferences in relation to memory and expectation. If micro-analysis is fundamental then this has implications for epistemology and conceptual analysis, and in particular for their sceptical wing, which needs to be balanced by an anti-sceptical wing if the bird is to fly.

Consider the epistemological question, starting with misconceptions about memory. Imagine that I recall a childhood birthday party during which I scoffed most of the cakes, the memory images fresh in my mind as if recently baked. Then it would be a mistake to assume that the remembered event causes the memory and grounds it. It may or may not cause it, and no doubt this is of psychological interest—but not in any philosophical context in which epistemic scepticism is on the prowl, as in the present case. For one cannot ground the birthday memory in its causal connection with the birthday event, which very obviously would be to beg the question. One is faced with two apparently separate beliefs turning out to be a compound belief. The first is that I attended a birthday party; the second is that the birthday event caused the first; which is thereby contained in the second.

What is also misguided is the belief, or perhaps vague impression, that memory provides direct epistemic access to the event remembered. This it cannot do, or not in the everyday sense, and arguably this notion of direct access is incoherent. In what way, then, is memory belief justified? One response would be to appeal to confirmation, for instance if I ask someone I believe to have been a fellow guest at the party whether she remembers my being there and loading my plate with cakes. But now, if my memory of the party is under review, and for no reason except that the past is not a place but a state of non-existence, so that possibly my seeming memory is false, then the very idea of confirmation is without application. For processes of checking a particular memory depend at every stage on other memories, all of which would incriminate themselves as being evidentially unsupported in exactly the same way as the memory selected for interrogation. What I shall now establish is that extrapolation of this kind as a condition of being consistent is the key by which a solution to the problem is unlocked.

Enter, the door now opening, the notion of a system, within which I can doubt my memory of an event only by taking as veridical the memories by which the doubt finds expression. How can I be sure that I attended the party? I ask myself, and now I have to remember asking, this memory itself not in doubt. It follows that my reason for doubt cannot be such as to implicate the memories that enter into the doubt itself, otherwise I would have to doubt those memories, and the ensuing new memories, and so on.

By way of example, the birthday party guest who was asked to vouch for my presence at the party may disappoint by insisting that I was not there, in which case I may begin to doubt either my memory or his, depending on my attachment to one or the other, given this or that. Note, by the way, that a particular memory I am either confident or dubious about is able evidentially to confine these extremes within a small circle with itself at the centre. I simply feel one way or the other, this being its own reason, and that is all there is to it. The point being made is mainly that philosophical scepticism about memory refutes itself, for the sceptic relies on memory to make his case, by which he challenges *all* memory, and the same for expectation. Hence the self-refutation of dual or single scepticism of the kind in question. A subordinate point, taking a wider view, is that one's just *having* a belief—the circle again— is consonant with system-based analysis and the notion of the non-conscious as the engine room of consciousness.

## 2.1: Phenomenological Versus Intentional

My contention is that intentionality is generated in the non-conscious, this being connected with what I refer to as the myths of phenomenological and conscious adequacy, the former being treated first. The first step is to explain what is meant, initially in terms of the notion of memory. Suppose that I try to analyse what it is that recollective memory consists in. Perhaps I recall my cake scoffing at the party—or, rather, my cake-scoffing at the party; but the memory images as conscious phenomena, however vivid and aromatic, cannot constitute my memory of that occasion, not even when other memory images, attracted by the aroma, rush to the scene. For I might entertain such images in denying that the glutton was myself.

What, though, of the fact of phenomenal difference, for instance that between the images in the two cases? Or it may be that I falsely claim to remember the event, so that my saying 'I remember eating all the cakes.' will be experientially different. This is undoubtedly true, all the more so if a more salient example is given; namely, my uttering that or any other indicative sentence in English as compared with a non-Anglophone's experience of parroting the words. This difference is a significant one, manifesting as it does the distinction between meaning something and not meaning anything by the sentence; but it does not constitute the distinguishing of one from the other. I do not try to ascertain whether I give sense to the sentence by waiting to see which experience I have.

This is the approach I shall take when we pronounce upon intentionality in general, my aim in the interim being to demonstrate the facility with which that approach metaphysically resolves part of the puzzle of what it is that memory consists in. The reality, after all, is that the concept of the past is cognitively at the edge of everyday and philosophical understanding, tipping over as it does into intellectual anxiety paradoxically expressed. And all the more so, one might feel, if the misconceptions about memory that I earlier exposed are thereby removed. How can my memory of wolfing cakes, or wolfing the cakes, be so vivid, as if I am there, now, and yet so insubstantial, as if the past reduces to these pictured scenes and other ephemera of conscious recollection? There is, or so I claim, a partial answer in terms of the non-conscious, about which we shall now theorise to a limited therapeutic end.

Since, to begin with, all intentionality is a function of the non-conscious, this includes the intentional as it informs the concept of time. But if the non-conscious is unknowable, then there is a sense in which we do not know what we mean when we give meaning to a word. In that sense, whatever it may be, we do not know what the concept of time consists in. What we can surmise is that the workings of the non-conscious transcend temporal processes, in which case the paradoxicality of memory and the past as we understand them can at least be softened around the edges. My memory of the party all those decades ago is of an event that I registered by experiencing it, with all that this entails about the intentionality of the conscious processes involved. Since that intentionality manifested itself in consciousness and derived from the non-conscious, the same as my recollection, our contention is that past experience and present memory engage at the non-conscious level, this being the sense in which we may speak of access to the past across a span of time.

Let us now consider intentionality in general, this time in terms of a numerical example. Consider the relations between the intentional and the phenomenological as exhibited in my counting to 100. Suppose that I am numerate and understand the numbers. If queried on that point, I would say that 51 is the successor to 50 because $50+1=51$ and the sequence progresses in increments of 1.

If we zoom in on the sum 50+1=51, we may imagine that an innumerate person, call him Mr D, has learned how to pronounce "fifty plus one equals fifty-one". Perhaps he sounds just like me when he utters the words, but for him, or so we may imagine, they are empty sounds, as if belonging to a foreign language, which in a sense they do. Written down, too, they may look the same to him as to me. And yet, for me the sum is arithmetically meaningful, so that it is intentional; but for him it has no meaning. Then we may draw the conclusion that in myself but not in him the intentional in the arithmetical case penetrates to the non-conscious.

We now need to buttress the argument by defending it against criticisms, the first of which is that we have neglected the role of dispositions, the difference between Mr D and myself being that I am suitably disposed and he is not. Since this in itself is a neutral statement, it needs to be sharpened as follows. The dispositional difference is that I am disposed to issue further statements, perhaps by saying or writing that the sequence continues 52, 53…, and so on, or by solving sums. The problem here is that Mr D would not understand these arithmetical excursions and I would, which is to say that the criticism succeeds only in extending the difference between us.

Secondly, the theory may be criticised by comparison with the philosophy of Wittgenstein, whose claim about criteria and that the meaning of a word consists in its use is discussed in *Beyond Knowledge*, in particular with regard to statements about the past, which I argued conflict with it. A similar argument, it seems to me, can be used against the theory as applied to the arithmetical system. Just as, or so I claimed, statements about the past are used to describe past events, so it is that an arithmetical statement reports arithmetical facts, this being the use to which we put it, so that the implication is that we already understand it in our use of it. On my own theory an individual may engage in thought, including recollection, without giving any publicly understandable outward sign, for instance in my own slightly modified present case. It is true that I am both typing and thinking, but this would obtain even if no-one but myself understood English. What is missing is not shared public meaning, as if language has no subjective use, but the notion of the non-conscious, the role of which is that of communication with oneself—and with others. Last but not least, the theory that equates meaning with use does not lend itself to clarity, with not even a hint from its proponents, as far as I am aware, as to what it would entail in any particular case.

## 2.2: The Myth of Conscious Adequacy

How is the notion of the non-conscious to be anatomised? If the answer, or non-answer, is that it is inaccessible to enquiry, then we must ask how we know that it exists. Earlier I argued that it is the engine of the intentional, a fact that the phenomenology myth helps to conceal. The present argument will reference the myth of the adequacy of consciousness. Suppose again that a subject claims to be able to count to 100 and is already halfway up that hill. When he catches his breath at 50 we note that the previous forty-nine numbers are no longer conscious items, the number 50 itself in his mind only for a moment, so that we now have to account for and analyse his awareness of having recited the first fifty numbers. We know that he possesses that awareness, otherwise we would not expect him to utter "51" as the next number. We know, too, that he may be disposed to utter it, but a disposition is not a conscious event or process. It is true that it is actualised in consciousness, as when he recites the successor to "50", this being a conscious act; but the disposition is present between the saying of "50" and "51", just as it was in the step-by-step translon from "1" to "50". There must be a categorical source by which the numerical sequence is tracked, for the conscious acts in question are themselves inadequate as being constitutive of the intentionality involved.

My claim, then, is that consciousness is momentary, and that in this it is without limit. When I say "50" the first part of my utterance does not exist when I utter the second part, which itself does not survive being voiced. Without the non-conscious the second syllable might belong to a wide range of words with the same ending, such as "party" or "serendipity", or to non-words, such as "partypity". One would, however, have to be quick, for the final syllable is no sooner said than dead. Can we in some way depict what the absence of the non-conscious would be like?

Only, I believe, in some such way as the following. First find a quiet room in which to make yourself comfortable. Now close your eyes and let your stream of consciousness empty into the dullest of pools and then slow to a trickle. In the pool you have no choice but to be conscious; all the same, try not to be conscious *of* anything. Then this is what your vast reservoir of knowledge and of mental ability in all its forms would amount to—the sensation of being wet, which of course you could never articulate and, come to that, never experience, since a sensation has duration.

Still seeking clarity, imagine that I am looking at the sequence 1, 6, 15, 28 on a computer screen, with each number disappearing before its immediate successor is displayed. Now let a friend join me when the screen shows "28". Then we are both having much the same visual-number experience: that of seeing the number 28; but that is where the similarity ends. Recall that any phenomenal difference between us cannot constitute the cognitive difference; and note that there may be a considerable dispositional difference. One should not, however, be misled by this. For the cognitive difference cannot be defined as being dispositional, the reason for which is that a disposition is actualised in a conscious act or state—that is, phenomenally; but we know that the phenomenal is not the intentional, where this includes the cognitive.

None of this is to deny that one's dispositions and one's understanding are intimately connected. I may be disposed to, for instance, anticipate the computer program by writing "45" on a piece of paper as the next number, on the assumption that the *n*th term formula is quadratic and given by $2n^2 - n$. If my understanding of the sequence derives from the non-conscious, then so do my dispositions, their particular character determining the details of that understanding as consciously manifested. If consciousness is momentary, the intentionality it manifests cannot be explained by appeal to it, the myth of conscious adequacy thereby being exposed. One would not, after all, attempt to account for a computer screen display of the arithmetical sequence in terms that did not go beyond that display.

## 2.3: The Non-Conscious Under Fire

If we now anticipate possible objections to our postulating of the non-conscious, then one such, on behalf of science, is that the brain is the source of intention and the conscious mind. If we ask how it is that understanding a thing goes beyond the phenomenal, it will be said, then this is to be explained in terms of cerebral processes, which is what the non-conscious consists in. To this there are rejoinders, the first of which is that one's understanding of the brain's causal relationship with phenomenal consciousness itself goes beyond the conscious mind into the sphere of the intentional, which we have located in the non-conscious.

Secondly, neuroscience in its enquiries into the brain as the seat of consciousness reports only correlations between cerebral and conscious phenomena, this being all that its explanatory power amounts to. Finally, brain science poses no threat to our thesis about the myth of conscious adequacy, the exposing of which points directly to the existence of the non-conscious, which is therefore prior, in some sense, to the investigation of the correlations in question. The upshot is that the study of the nexus between the cerebral and the mental belongs to science, not to metaphysics, which transcends it.

Are there other criticisms of our theory of consciousness to be taken into account? So far, we have assumed that it is easy to distinguish between phenomenal and intentional, but some theorists take this to be a simplistic view of what is really a difficult distinction to make. To do justice to their stance, we shall examine an example of close reasoning in puzzle form in order to ascertain whether the intentionality involved is purely phenomenological.

Each of three men, one of them blind, has a hat placed on his head in such a way that he does not know its colour, though he knows that it has been selected from a set of three red hats and two black ones. Now each of the men is asked whether he knows the colour of his hat. The men are together and can see and hear one another, apart from the blind man, who can hear the other two. The first sighted man says he does not know; then the second sighted man says the same; then the blind man says yes, after listening to the other two he knows the colour of his hat. What is the colour of his hat and how does he know? To avoid the spoilers in the following paragraphs, it would be best to attempt a solution before reading on. If you attempt it mentally, not writing anything down, you will experience the effort of attentiveness about to be discussed.

It is given, then, that the blind man solves the puzzle by internal mental reasoning. His opening inference: 'For the first speaker to admit ignorance it must be that he can see that the second speaker and myself are not each wearing a black hat. If we were, then his would be red.' This first thought is deductive in character. As is the second, the problem thereby being solved: 'About the second speaker: if I have a black hat, then his must be red, since we cannot both have black hats. But he admits ignorance after hearing the first speaker, therefore my hat is red.'

We are supposing that the blind man has made an effort to retain in his mind his conclusion about the first man while reasoning about the second. What would a critic of the thesis of the non-conscious believe about the blind man's mental processes? He would say that these are conscious processes that depend not at all on the workings of a supposed non-conscious entity that operates beneath the surface of consciousness. If they did so dep-end, he might say, then how would the fact of concentrated mental exertion fit into that conceptual scheme? Clearly, the blind man's cogitations about the second man depend on his retaining in consciousness, or bringing back into it, his prior reasoning; but why should that be the case if his thoughts derive from the non-conscious?

Let us agree that this is a point to be considered, not only in brain science but also in metaphysics. In the former, however, the critic's argument would be rejected, the non-conscious being equated with processes in the brain. Since, that said, the neuroscientist would not be able to account for the mental effort in question, there is no reason why the metaphysician should not admit to the same defeat. It is not as if, after all, one professes to be able to explain the phenomena to which the critic draws attention, of which there are many more, I am sure, that similarly have questions attached.

In philosophy more generally, too, there are connected issues, in particular that of epiphenomenalism, according to which there are no conscious causal processes, a theory that is both interesting and counter-intuitive. If I accidentally place my hand in a flame, whereupon I scream and jerk my hand away, then it may seem to me with certainty that my pain caused me to react in that way, a thesis that the epiphenomenalist rejects. Note that if she is correct, then without exception there are no causal sequences of conscious events, in which case the blind man's mental efforts would seem to be inexplicable, as indeed would my feeling pain if it has a cause but no effect, which is to say that it is epiphenomenal.

What are we to make of this form of scepticism? If it is indeed counter-intuitive, then so are the theories that arguably entail it, namely that of the non-conscious and that of the brain as the source of consciousness. Perhaps, then, I should go with the flow and embrace the epiphenomenal if the theory of the non-conscious is to keep its head above water. The problem here, however, is that counter-intuitiveness continues to be an im-pediment that the currents of the theory must negotiate.

Is there, perhaps, an alternative approach? Indeed there is, and it resolves the problem. We know that the concept of cause and effect has itself been caught up in the rapids of philosophical controversy since at least the time of Hume, who was mainly responsible for sending it over the edge, the only buoyant part being that of the constant conjunction of events. We know, too, that neuropsychology and brain science in general investigate correlations between brain structure and processes and particular forms of consciousness. And, again, that on this more relaxed construal of causation we may adduce much in the way of regular connection between conscious events or states and physical behaviour or action. For instance, we jerk our hand away from pain, itself an effect of the flame via bodily processes, including those that are cerebral. Indeed, the whole of the sub-system of psychological explanation feeds on itself in just this way, the mental or behavioural explaining the mental or behavioural or itself being thus explained, as when I observe that in reading Christopher Hitchens' *Mortality*, I cried, which made my partner cry, at which point I stopped, though I still felt upset, as did she, and we embraced in sorrow.

Does that relaxation itself need justifying? Hume has done most of the work, but note, not necessarily against him, since he is open to interpretation, that the very fact of the existence of that explanatory sub-system demands that we breathe more freedom into the concept of cause and effect if we are to inflate that system from its everyday and scientific application to the level of philosophical respectability. Either that or we challenge Hume, but the more we succeed, if at all, the more problematic the system becomes.

Since this cannot be right, I find myself yet again upholding the conceptual status quo—or, more nuanced, insisting that our task is that of analysis not rejection, quite possibly in line with Hume, depending on one's exegetical stance, but in any case in line with a sceptical version of common sense. There is nothing ordinarily commonsensical about theorising a realm of the unknowable non-conscious into existence. But note that it transcends common sense rather than directly threatens it.

That leaves the myth of conscious adequacy to weave into the scheme of the intentional non-conscious, this being the section in which I canvass theorists of consciousness for their views. Before then, I have a few remarks to make, mostly by way of linking the present section with the previous one. In defending the thesis of the non-conscious by appeal to the myth of phenomenological adequacy, I could also have enlisted the myth of the adequacy of consciousness in support, as I did initially in arguing for that thesis. The two approaches are complementary and also stand alone. Still, it is important to be able to call upon both of them, linked as they are in several ways. There is one link in particular that we need to follow, and it concerns conscious continuity, this being the point at which I consult other commentators.

In *The Self*, edited by Galen Strawson, Barry Dainton criticises what he refers to as '*The Cut Argument*', his aim being to defend the notion of the continuity of stream of consciousness. The argument starts from the observation that if we die, the cessation of consciousness affects its last moments not at all, for they do not know, as it were, that they are the last, and after they have come and gone they cannot be affected by anything, for they are past events. For Dainton it would then follow that stream of consciousness consists phenomenally of self-contained, isolated experiential episodes, any continuity of consciousness thereby being precluded. Given the undoubted fact of continuity, he says, the argument must be flawed. Placing its flaws on hold for the moment, let us review the reasoning by which they were detected.

Is it really true that a stretch of experience 'could be just as it is, phenomenologically speaking, if the experiences before and after it did not exist'? (p.12) That depends, for if, for instance, my experience at time $t$ is of riding a horse, and if at time $t$ minus a few seconds the horse collapsed and died, then at time $t$ I would be falling, not riding. Since I am riding, not falling, the horse did not collapse and die.

The point is a very general one: if successive events A, B and C occur, then it is trivially true that they permit or enable one another to exist, and in particular that B is existentially compatible with A and C. If it is to make sense to say, as quoted, that B could exist even if A and C did not exist, then the meaning must be such as to render irrelevant the possibility that B relies causally on A, since Dainton does not mention it. What must be meant is that if B occurs and is preceded by A, then it remains the case that B occurs; and the same if C succeeds B, at which point Dainton refers to there being no such thing as backward causation. That, however, is not pertinent and indeed is impertinent, for if B occurs then it occurs, this being a tautology and nothing to do with causation. Note as before that our reasoning in terms of events translates easily into the counterpart account in terms of the corresponding experiences.

All that Dainton's construal of the cut argument has delivered so far, then, is logical truism; and yet, he reads into it the implication that a stream of consciousness would lack the continuity that it undeniably exhibits; therefore the cut argument is flawed. There is no such implication, and the argument is not so much flawed as vacuous. That said, it is worth examining the flaws in the argument according to Dainton, who illustrates them as follows. Suppose, he says, that a pianist repeatedly plays the scale C-D-E-F-G-A-B-C..., which is heard in full by a normal individual, call him Mr Long, but only the D is heard, and for two seconds, by an individual who lives only for that space of time, call him Mr Short. Dainton acknowledges that the hearing of D may be the same for both listeners, and also the memory-image of C and expectation of E. This is odd, given that Mr Short hears only the D, but let it pass. The significant auditory difference says Dainton, resides in the 'diachronic phenomenal relations' (p. 13), such that only Mr Long hears C-running into D and D into E. Time, I think, to sharpen the critical notes.

To begin with, we are to assume that they both hear the same two-second D note, but only Mr Long—and the pianist—hear the C morphing into it and it into E. That is, they objectively hear the same sound, but phenomenally only Mr Long relates D to C and E, and by way of auditory transition. This is problematic on more than one count—perhps two. For we are also told that both listeners may have the experience of the memory of C and expectation of E, in which case one might ask how this is different from the transition experience. Not that it matters much, for the fact is, in any case, that it is logically possible for Mr Short to have exactly the same experience as Mr Long, for all that Dainton has shown to the contrary.

A further fact, as we have already established, is that the cut argument does not pose a threat to the continuity of consciousness, nor, indeed, to anything else. Keep in mind, too, that the notion of conscious continuity is more muddled than clear, as also that the fact of interruptedness, as when we sleep, is itself enough to muddy the muddle, so that the first step would be to try to clarify what might be meant. We do not need to, which is probably a good thing.

Bringing the present section to an end, my stated aim was to look further into the non-conscious by way of the myth of conscious adequacy, this to be achieved by appraising the views of those who would disagree with me. Dainton's focus, as we have just seen, is on phenomenology, an approach that thereby makes itself vulnerable to criticism. One is always mistaken, in my view, if the claim is that certain experiences logically constrain others, or constrain the associated concepts. I argued in our discussion of Molyneux' problem that it may be empirically the case that a perceiver acquires a perceptual concept only on the basis of the right kind of sensory experience. But the necessity is contingent; for it is always logically possible that the perceiver's brain be in the state that it would have been in if the experience had occurred. Similarly, it is logically possible that Mr Short's brain be in the state it would have been in had he enjoyed the full musical experience of the scales, or at least of C, D and E, by which Mr Long was privileged.

Turning to the cut argument, it misses a trick by being blind to the fact that if you take short intervals of consciousness, you can demonstrate that it is momentary, which leads directly to the non-conscious. The argument, on Dainton's interpretation, focusses on the phenomenal, which is expected to do the work that by right should be undertaken by the non-conscious. This will also become apparent in the chapters on perception, the first of which is next.

# Chapter 3: The Problem of Perception

The problem of perception is one of the most daunting of all the philosophical problems that are easy to explain but seemingly impossible to solve. Its intractability arises from two glaringly obvious facts about what it is to perceive, both of them apparently beyond question yet utterly opposed to each other. One such fact is that the senses present as our playground an objectively real perception-independent external world which includes our bodies, brains and sense organs. Thus it is that we are able to skip among the swings, roundabouts and see-saws and confirm at every step, the epitome of epistemic superfluity, that we inhabit a three-dimensional physical space, admittedly with its ups and downs but undeniably the world in which we live.

The other fact, equally unassailable if certain assumptions are made, is that the deliverances of our senses, suitably construed, are wholly subjective, with not even the sense of sight an exception to the rule. An exemplar in this regard is the auditory sense, for instance if we say that we hear a skylark, an observation that becomes more subjective if rendered as 'I hear a trilling sound which leads me to believe, in relation to its external source, that there is a skylark in the vicinity.' But listening to a trilling sound, on the present construal, is a subjective experience like any other, notwithstanding the fact that I hear the sound as being out there in the world. For although facts of the "perceiving as" kind are of interest in the philosophy of perception, they do not, again when suitably construed, detract from the perceptual subjectivity that is our present concern. It is also one of the concerns of the sceptic about perception, who issues the following provocation. That if sensory experience in general is like audition in being wholly subjective, then the external world collapses into the personal realm of the subjectively perceptual, at least insofar as anything that extreme can be conceived of.

But is it really true, despite our initial claims as to the glaringly obvious, that perception is wholly subjective? I entered a caveat, after all, about its needing to be suitably construed, for what does "subjective" mean? If we consider the sense of taste or smell, then the sceptic may contend that it is essentially similar to a sensation—and we do, indeed, speak of gustatory or olfactory sensations. Note that we cannot dismiss this assimilation by simply claiming that smell or taste may be observationally informative; for a toothache may inform us dentally, and the ebb and flow of chest pain may alert us to an impending tsunami. And now the sceptic may contend that sight, hearing and touch are essentially similar to these other two senses. His point is that any sensory information on the crest of an auditory, visual or tactual wave will spill over into further subjective sense experience. Hearing a trilling sound, I expect a visual experience as of seeing a skylark.

If such experience does not reach beyond itself and open a window onto the external world, then clearly it cannot be shared with other people, of whom there would be none, this being a serious problem for a solipsistic socialite. That being the case, a subjectivist theory of perception is eminently dismissable as being too preposterous to be seriously entertained. It may be brought back to reality if the window of perception is opened again, the light from outside flooding in.

There is, after all, the fact of "perceiving as" which configures itself along the lines of the intentional, in particular with regard to vision, which is more resistant than audition to being contorted into the Procrustean bed of the phenomenal. Imagine looking at a text and trying, instead of reading it, to see it as a sequence of shapes. Or, for that matter, hearing someone speak English and trying not to understand it; or listening to a trilling sound as if directly overhead and willing oneself not to expect a skylark if one looks up. Intentionality is clearly involved in hearing spoken sounds as words, and perhaps less obviously in hearing trilling sounds as birdsong. The phenomenal and intentional are not always distinct enough to be sharply differentiated, this being one of the obstacles to clear thinking in this arena. Another is that perceptual experience is intrinsic to perception, including to perceiving as, so that we are back with subjective and objective and cannot eliminate either of them. Therefore, any theory of perception must not only accommodate but also reconcile them, at least within limits.

One of the gains we have made is that we now have a criterion for seriously entertaining a theory of perception: that it should not entail absurdity, the subjectivist thesis thereby being ruled out. Its place will be taken, in due course, by a system-based approach to perception in which full justice is done to its intentionality. We shall then return to the apparent conflict between the subjective and objective standpoint, together with the perplexity thus engendered, one of our aims being to establish the legitimacy of this latter within a system. Hence the mention just now of limits.

At this point one should note that all reasoning, insofar as it is conscious, is mediated by subjective awareness, as when we work out a puzzle or recollect a past event or engage in philosophy. I am now telling myself that if all A is B, then all not-B is not A, assistance being provided by the mental image I have of a little circle, A, inside another circle, B. This is abstract Aristotelian logic, expressing as it does a syllogistic truth that impinges not at all on anything objective—and yet it is logically certain at the same time as it is wholly subjective. Even so, we do not find it problematic on that account.

Having made a note and expressed an interest, it is now time for a new departure, our mission being to critically examine a more traditional perceptual scepticism, central to which is the argument from illusion. Before saddling up, however, we should perhaps relate that argument to the present discussion, the connection being as follows. Firstly, a sceptical theory of perception cannot entail solipsism or threaten the basic tenets of the everyday school of thought by which the physical world reveals itself as objectively real and existing unperceived. A theory that excludes other people from existence cannot overcome one's countervailing certainties, in particular with regard to friends and family. The dehumanising of those we keep close would necessitate a change from "whom" to "which" that all concerned would find upsetting. Even to apologise to them for having to maintain one's integrity as a sceptic would be self-refuting, which is to say that one's intellectual integrity would either give the lie to itself or would be taken to indicate insanity.

Philosophy should not be taken to license tilting at windmills, especially when one recognises them for what they are, any claims to the contrary being little more than pretence. There is no point in saddling up an armchair when it is obviously not a horse and cannot be ridden as one. The case of rocking horses, I admit, is not so clearcut.

## 3.1: Scepticism Confronted

If we now turn to the argument from illusion, I propose to consider it in relation to its treatment in A.D.Smith's *The Problem of Perception*. Smith is of the view that the argument is not taken seriously enough, a defect which he rectifies in the book; and his aim is the modest one of meeting this challenge to direct realism, leaving open the possibility that it can be attacked from other directions. He sets out the argument in some detail, but broadly speaking the first step is to establish the existence of illusions, and the second is to introduce what he refers to as the sense-datum inference, which runs as follows. If, with regard to what seems to be a limited class of perceptible features, namely those that are basic, an object appears to a perceiver to exhibit such a feature but in reality does not, then that feature, or apparent feature, is nevertheless instantiated in his perceptual experience of the object.

Using Smith's example, if a white wall looks yellow to me, where yellow is a basic feature or sensible quality, then *something* is yellow, the reference being to a sense datum. We now have the sense datum inference, for instance with regard to colour, according to which the immediate objects of one's colour awareness in cases of perceptual illusion are not the physical surfaces in which the colours seem to inhere; rather, one is directly aware of non-physical sense data which exist or occur only when perceived.

Taking a further step, Smith now presents the sense-datum infection thesis, which again applies to all the senses. It states that if some features of an object are illusory, so that our direct awareness is of sense data, then this is true of all features of the object in that sense field. Using vision as an example, he points out that the shape of an object is defined by the pattern of colour it presents; therefore, if its colour is illusory then so is its shape. Thus, if the yellow appearance of a white wall is a sense datum, then so is the shape of the wall, one's visual experience of the wall being of sense data and nothing else.

The final step is that in which the sense-datum inference is generalised to cover veridical as well as illusory perception. What lends itself to this extension is the claim that illusory perception may be phenomenally indistinguishable from perceptual experience of real as opposed to illusory features of the physical world. Smith asks us to imagine that an article of clothing we examine under coloured lights in a shop looks very different when we bring it outside, where its true colour is revealed. How could it be, he asks, that our visual experience of the article suddenly changes from direct awareness of sense data to directly seeing a physical object? Thus it is, according to Smith, that the argument from illusion presents a serious challenge to direct realism.

Still concerned to reinforce the argument before attacking it from the particular direction he has in mind, he now takes issue with the defence of direct realism mounted by those he refers to as New Realists, who deny the validity of the third step of the argument. Their contention is that in many cases of illusion the illusory feature attaches to the object in the same way as its "real" features, so that it has ontological parity with them. Thus, a straight stick looking bent in water is a publicly observable phenomenon, as is a white wall looking yellow if suitably illuminated. These visual appearances are explicable in terms of the behaviour of light and the properties of the bodies it acts upon, none of which involves defective eyesight or changes in the perceiver's visual apparatus.

The thesis thus illustrated is that in such cases, those in which so-called perceptual illusion has a physically objective basis or explanation, the illusory features are just as genuine as those that we certify as real. It is clear that Smith is drawn to this way of dealing with the problem, at least when it is not taken too far, though he does suggest that even with moderate new realism the everyday distinction between the apparent and the real would have to be revised. After all, he says, one would not normally agree that changing a light bulb alters the colours of objects lit by it. Still, he thinks the revision might be worth making if the thesis in question could be shown to be universally applicable to perceptual illusion.

In fact, he thinks that this cannot be shown, and indeed that many cases of illusion are rooted in psychology or physiology, so that they are subjective in character. By way of example, he adduces the fact that the apparent colour of an object may change if it is juxtaposed with contrasting colours; and, too, when a colour-blind person sees a red object as green, this is not because of any change in the object itself or in the processes by which it is illuminated. Subjective illusions also occur, or conceivably could occur, in the case of the other senses, he thinks, and for this and other reasons he rejects the new realists' proposed solution to the problem of perception. He does not consider the view that even with subjective illusion a physical explanation can always be found, as in the case of colour blindness. Neither, or so it seems, does he detect anti-sceptical significance in the fact that perceptual illusions arise only within a framework of veridical perception.

Smith now suggests that the only way to defeat the illusion argument is to challenge the sense-datum inference itself; in other words the reasoning by which the sceptic infers from the fact of illusion to the existence of sense data or other perceptual proxies, these being taken to be immediate objects of perception. As before, Smith again plays devil's advocate, this time by emphasising the strength of that inference in its role as the main support of the argument from illusion. 'When something appears yellow to me', he says, 'it is, or could be, with me visually just as it is when I veridically see something that really is yellow. The same "sensible quality" is present to consciousness in the two cases.'(p.36) He says that the aim of the illusion argument is to bring us to the recognition that *'sensible qualities can be present to consciousness in perception despite the fact that they do not characterise the normal physical objects we are said to be perceiving.'*(p.37)

This is unclear, partly because the notion of a sensible quality seems to be both subjective and objective. If sense-datum theory is correct, then a sensible quality which one takes to attach to a physical object also seems to attach to the sense datum one is immediately aware of when perceiving the object. A difficulty here is that if sense data are mind-dependent, existing or occurring only when perceived, then they are intimately linked to the phenomenal aspect of perceptual experience, to what it is to see, hear, smell and so on, whereas a sensible quality regarded as a physical feature of an object exists independently and unperceived. A separation of semantic roles is required and Smith now follows others in letting "sensible quality" have a physical reference and introducing the term "sensory quality" to apply to the basic features attaching to sense data.

## 3.2: Are Sense Data Real?

This is not, one might think, a very successful clarifying move, given that a sensory quality of yellow, say, would seem to be a sufficiency unto itself, the sensible quality of yellow thereby made redundant. Our visual sense, after all, picks up only the sensory quality. Prior to further criticism along these lines, however, I suggest that the notion of a sense datum is itself obscure, not to mention incoherent, a thesis for which a variety of arguments will be advanced. To begin with, Smith's claim on behalf of the sceptic is that illusory sensory qualities must attach to something, namely to sense data, these being regarded as the bearers of both illusory and veridical such qualities. But this is to imply, or is confusedly taken to imply, that a sense datum has a separate identity from that of sensory qualities. Different instances of it may attach to it on different occasions, an analogous case being that in which a post box retains its identity when painted a different colour. On that analogy, we are entitled to ask what the properties of a sense datum might be in virtue of which it can vary in sensory quality. Thus, a red and a blue sense datum successively experienced fall into the category of entities rather than events, this distinction being such as to permit the sense data to be one and the same, apart from the difference in colour.

It would seem that there are no such properties, and this hardens into certainty if, as is traditional, or intrinsic to their definition, we regard sense data as perception-dependent, so that they lack numerical identity. Such dependence does not entail, according to some commentators, that they are mental, and Smith appears to believe that they are not; but clearly they are not physical, so that the point about numerical identity still stands.

That leaves qualitative identity, and if this comes into play, as with a wall looking yellow on separate occasions, then we may see fit to ascribe that yellowness to a sense datum, in other words to say that this is a visual sense datum and that its colour is yellow. Again, then, a question arises as to the way in which the sense datum is distinct from the sensory quality of yellow. At the level of grammar the answer is obvious, for the sense datum is the subject and "yellow" is the predicate, this being just one of a range of sensory qualities predicated of sense data.

Subject-predicate sentence construction, however, wherein the subject is capable of ranging over a variety of predicates, need indicate not at all the presence of an entity distinct from its attributes, in the sense that it is able to survive at least *some* change in them. This is numerical identity, as with the post box being painted different colours; but qualitative identity belongs in a different category, at least for present purposes. If, for instance, we say in standard subject-predicate form, 'the colour of this wall is yellow', then yellow is an instance of colour, not something attributed to it, for 'colour' is a generic term for a range of visual features belonging to a natural kind, the predicate in the sentence picking out one of them. Ontologically, nothing would be lost if we said simply that the wall is yellow. In what way, then, is a sense datum something over and above the sensory qualities by which it is described? Not, or so I have argued, in the way that the identity of a post box transcends its particular colour. We know, however, that proponents of sense-datum theory posit a bearer of illusory sensory qualities, this being a sense datum since it cannot be a physical object. But why should it be anything at all? Not only is the notion of a sense datum problematic but on a neutral view it is also unnecessary. Dispensing with it, we could simply say that in illusory cases sensory qualities are instantiated in experience, the claim then being made that sometimes they are indistinguishable from their counterparts in veridical cases. We should now ask whether, on the sense-datum view, a distinction between veridical and illusory cases can any longer be made. But for the moment we are enquiring into the classification of colours.

The fact is, after all, that it would be better if we could make enquiries without the impediment of a spurious class of entities. And, too, it would be conducive to that enquiry if we were more alert to how easily subject-predicate sentence construction, especially if it involves technical terms, or everyday terms given a technical twist, can turn grammatical subject into ontological substance – and best of all is that it proceeds, as it were, by linguistic stealth, this being the method, arguably, by which the notion of sense data insinuates itself into the debate about perceptual realism.

If this is acknowledged, so that at best the point of sense-datum terminology is to facilitate discourse rather than to make an existential claim, then to speak of sense data is to re-describe in compact form the state of affairs in which the introduction of such terms was originally grounded. If we eschew the use of those terms, because even in their facilitative role they lead us astray, then what remains to us is to speak instead of sensory qualities, except that although this is arguably less misleading than talk of sense data, it is not necessarily more perspicuous, the notion of sensory qualities having problems of its own. It has its warrant, as we know, in the fact of illusory and veridical perception being subjectively identical, as with seeing a white wall as yellow in exactly the way that one sees a yellow wall. This, as we have seen, is where the difficulty lies; and it could be, that apart, that one's conceptual apparatus is already equipped to deal with such cases, the language of appearance enabling us to speak of the way things look, in this instance a wall looking yellow. Again, then, the same as with sense data, we are entitled to ask a question: in what way does the concept of a sensory quality improve upon or differ from that of perceptual appearance?

The basic difficulty, one which we keep encountering, is that of aligning sense data and their associates with the distinction between perceptual consciousness and its objects in the physical world. Some would say that no such alignment is possible, and that this is as it should be, for sense data are posited as being neither physical nor mental; rather, they constitute the material from which physical and mental reality is constructed. What I suggest, however, is that this metaphysical scheme, known as neutral monism, does too great an injury to our system of perceptual concepts for it ever to be brought under the discipline of coherent and convincing theory. More particularly a sense datum as usually conceived lacks the perception independence by which physical objects are characterised.

My point is that even if the argument from illusion raises a serious sceptical issue, it cannot be resolved by the conjuring up of an ontological realm, neither physical nor mental, inhabited by sense data and sensory qualities. These notions gain content disjointedly from established perceptual concepts. We are told that if a white wall looks yellow to me, I am aware of a yellow sense datum. But one should not be misled by this use of "aware", for my visual experience is as of looking at a yellow wall, this being attended by perceptual beliefs all of which may be correct, even if this means that I have to say not that the wall is yellow but that it looks yellow to me. None of this involves sense data or the belief that they obtain, which would – or should – conflict with my belief that I see a physical object, even if its apparent colour is not its real colour in the sense of being the colour it standardly exhibits. I say "should" in recognition of sense data being taken to be non-physical, for the wall's colour cannot be both physical and non-physical; hence the conflict.

In practice, however, this being where the illicit content insinuates itself, one tries to find sense even where none exists, such that the attempt to reconcile opposites leads to cognitive disarray. That is, we try to see the yellow colour as external to us and occupying the same space in our visual field as the wall, but abstracted from it rather than inhering in its physical surface. This results in incoherence, and in any case the sense-datum theory would apply not just to colour but also to physical space itself, so that there would be no physical surface for the colour yellow to abstract itself from.

What is a sense datum supposed to be? To show that it cannot be neutral between mental and physical, consider again the auditory sense, again using birdsong as an example. Then my hearing a trilling sound is pure auditory consciousness, a mental state, even if it involves "hearing as", in this case hearing a sound sequence as the song of a skylark. Keep in mind that a sense-datum theorist is touchingly innocent of any notion of perceptual intentionality. It would have to be, given these conditions, that auditory sense data are mental; but now it is obvious that they equate with auditory experience itself, so that they add nothing to our understanding of what it is to hear a thing. Indeed, they subtract from it, neglecting as they do the realm of the perceptually intentional.

None of this is to deny, with regard to perception, that there is a need for analysis, for instance of the concept of physical reality as applied selectively to an object's apparent features, as with the description of a yellow-looking wall as really being white. But this is not the same as needing to answer sceptical objections to perceptual realism. To be able to eliminate them, however, we do need to answer them, the place to start being with Locke's theory of perception, which in some respects is both sceptical and metaphysical.

## 3.3: Primary and Secondary Qualities

It has been shown that if we focus on the sensory colour quality when looking at a post box, then instead of a red physical object we have what it is like to see it, as if the red surface of the box has become detached and turned into the subjective seeing of red. This is far too obscure and misleading, and in any case it is an incorrect account of what it is that perceptual introspection reveals. The corrected picture now presented, if the aim is to achieve perceptual verisimilitude, is of visually registering a red post box as both subjective and objective. For I see the post box as a red object out there in the world and in so doing, I experience its redness, the whole process being seamless unless I reflect on it. Upon reflection I realise that I cannot separate the subjective experience of red from the seeing of the red surface of the box; and now I have to enquire into the implications of this unsettling inability. Does it imply that my perceptual experience delivers not a physical world but only further such experience? But that would be the extreme solipsism that we have condemned as being preposterous; and the stance we are taking is that if a course is plotted for that particular maelstrom, then very likely the ship will spiral to the bottom of the sea.

If the distinction between sensible and sensory qualities is problematic, given their failure to engage gears, then the grinding of cogs will be further pronounced if we now consider what Smith has to say about another distinction: that between primary and secondary qualities in Locke's theory of perception. On that theory primary qualities of shape, size and motion belong to the structure of the physical world, whereas secondary qualities of colour, taste, smell and so on are subjective in their effects. This is to say that the physical properties of an object, the reference being to sensible qualities, determine the qualitative character of our perceptual experience of it, this being a reference to sensory qualities. Thus, a standard post box, though not itself coloured, or not as the layman takes it to be, has objective properties such as to cause, or to be disposed to cause, one's visual experience of the colour red when looking at the box.

If we now ask about the relation between "sensible quality" and "primary quality", we find that they cannot be equated, for sensible qualities include both colour and shape, as with Smith's reference to an object's looking red and round. But shape, according to Locke, is a primary quality and colour is a secondary quality. What this indicates, in my view, is that Locke's theory is untenable, this being a conclusion deducible from the fact that colour defines shape, as also from the implausibility of the Lockean thesis about secondary qualities. Taking this latter first, we are invited to believe that to see the coloured surface of a physical object, as common sense would phrase it, is to have a visual experience such as is produced in us by a property or disposition of the physical object. This, as it stands, is truistic, for we already know, albeit in a qualified way and involving inference, that perceptual experience is externally caused by its objects, just as we know that we are aware of that experience.

What is needed, if the secondary quality thesis is to be of interest, is that it should imply that the everyday belief that colour inheres in physical objects, foisted onto us by the phenomenology of seeing, is erroneous or in need of re-formulation. It is hard to see what this latter would entail, and as for the possibility of error, this would mean that our seeing colours as inhering in objects is misleading and incorrect. It is true, of course, that in seeing colours we experience them, as also that it would be a category mistake to ascribe colour experience, rather than the colour itself, to an object; hence the suggestion, analogical in nature, that vision is transparent to the physical world. This aligns itself with the counter-intuitive nature of the secondary quality colour thesis, the evidence for which, if it is to target colour but not shape, would have to be both subtle and compelling.

As for what that evidence is, all that Smith vouchsafes to us is that the primary/secondary quality distinction is required if the argument from illusion is to be defeated. Perhaps we are to take it that the argument proves that colours are subjective, with shapes avoiding this ontological demolition only if the distinction at issue comes to their rescue. In fact, it cannot save them, for the argument covers shape as well as colour, as with the immersed part of a stick looking bent. Not only that, but Smith seems to concede, as we have seen, that in many instances illusory colours are publicly observable, as indeed are illusory shapes, which leaves only such cases as those of colour blindness. But this, in line with earlier remarks, is an optical aberration which in terms of the science of vision is well understood, the same being true of such phenomena as a stick looking bent in water, so that arguably they should be treated the same in terms of the argument from illusion.

One of my aims, in any case, is to show at a deeper level, that at which perceptual processes operate within a system, that the sceptical arguments in question are misconceived, for in the contrast they make between normal and deviant perception they take as deviant those features which are all-pervasive, such as that the appearance of an object depends on the relevant conditions. That being the case, these features belong to the theory of direct realism and cannot be used against it. Thus it is that we have been able to show that the secondary quality thesis is incoherent and lacks cogency, both in itself and in its implications. Time, then, to move on.

## 3.4: Towards Perceptual Intentionality

My disagreement with Smith revolves around the perceptually intentional, his neglect of which, or so it seems to me, reduces the senses to organs of sensation. Smith, on the other hand, claims that his phenomenological approach accommodates phenomenal intentionality, in which case we need to make its nature clear. One example is that of seeing a physical object as having spatial depth, which in some sense is integral to the visual experience itself; another is that of hearing a sound as located in external space, which is also where we take felt objects to be. What needs to be asked, then, is whether phenomenal intentionality is immediately given, in the sense of being non-inferential, in line with Smith's phenomenological approach. Since I have already answered that question in *Beyond Knowledge*, I shall now repeat what I wrote more or less verbatim.

Consider again what it is to hear a trilling sound, but this time without trying to prune it hard back to a sensation. I hear the sound, in some sense, as being external to my body, unlike tinnitus, the difference between them, with regard to the auditory experience itself, being traceable, according to Smith, to its phenomenal character As for what it is that the actual experience of phenomenal intentionality consists in, imagine a trilling sound heard by two people, one of them an ornithologist and the other newly emerged from a subterranean existence, this being the first time for her to see the sky, let alone locate a sound in it. Clearly, their experience of the sound might be different, the troglodyte not hearing it as external to her body, and not in any case as birdsong.

The crucial point is that phenomenal intentionality is perceptually significant only within a system, one in which intentionality of that kind, as indeed in general, manifests itself in the interplay between those experiences that either exhibit it or occur within a framework in which it is exhibited. Such interplay takes the form of actual or dispositional relations between and within perceptual experiences. Thus the ornithologist, as compared with the troglodyte, may have a different auditory experience and in any case is differently disposed in any of a multitude of ways, each of them, if realised, involving further occurrent and dispositional differences. If we focus on perception as a process, rather than as an isolated perceptual act, this latter being very much the way that Smith treats it, then it is clear that some dispositions are always realised, which is to say, in the present case, that the differences between the two observers may become increasingly more occurrent and actual.

The ornithologist's experience of the trilling sound may be more informative, especially if he cocks his head, a habit he picked up from birds, all the better to attune himself to distance and direction, whereupon he shields his eyes from the sun and scans a particular region of the sky. The troglodyte, meanwhile, listens to the trilling sound for itself and appreciates its insistent cheerfulness. If the ornithologist is able to spot the skylark, he perhaps describes it as a black speck in blue space, or as an amorphous blur, which nevertheless is the still centre of such clarity of song. It is a distant object, too tiny to exhibit spatial depth, but embedded in a voluminous sky. This illustrates the reference just now to objects either exhibiting phenomenal intentionality or being located in a framework which does exhibit it, as is always the case with objects in the physical world.

If phenomenal intentionality belongs within a system, then it should be possible to demonstrate this by tracking the effect on it of changes to that system, thereby revealing its necessary conditions of operation. Take, for instance, the way in which hearing a sound is perceptual by virtue of apparent externality and of conveying information about the distance and direction of its physical source, which it does via the phenomenon of "hearing as". Suppose that the signposts embedded in auditory experience become increasingly unreliable, pointing haphazardly this way and that. Listening to the song of a skylark, I now scan a particular region of the sky, only to find that in fact the skylark hovers in a different region farther away. Now imagine that phenomenological misdirection of this kind becomes the rule rather than the exception, so that even if the phenomenon of "hearing as" remains in place, no attention is paid to it as yielding information about its physical source. This in effect is to say that hearing loses its perceptual status as one of the primary senses, the others being sight and touch.

Continuing in the same vein, let us now consider links being weakened not between hearing and the other senses but within the same sense modality, this time using vision as an example. Suppose that the trilling heard earlier comes from a pet skylark and that I call it down from the sky, noticing as it homes in on me that it seems unsteady in flight. Perched on my finger, it displays the near side of its body, which I see as a curved surface, one which points, as it were, to its continuation both under and over the visible part of the bird to its far side. Suppose, however, that when I adjust the skylark's position, bringing its hitherto unseen side more into view, I discover–that which, amazingly, had escaped my notice–that it is flat. This explains the skylark's erratic mode of flying, and it illustrates the intimate connection between perception and inference or expectation.

If the bird's far side is flat, its near side being curved, then it must be that the boundary between them, both over and under, coincides exactly with that between the visible part of the near side and the unseen part of the far side relative to my field of view. But that would be sheer coincidence, it being much more likely that the visible curved surface is not the whole of it, which is to say that it continues out of sight, in line with my knowing as a general fact that birds typically have round bodies.

Suppose, however, that such knowledge, insofar as it is derived from vision, came increasingly under threat, as would be the case if visual prediction became wholly unreliable, one act of seeing no longer indicative of another. Here I have in mind not just expectations as to curved surfaces but much more generally the myriad ways in which inference enters into perception, the scope of which goes beyond anything that could conceivably be regarded as being immediately given in sense-experience. Looking at the jumble of books on this table, some of them partially hidden under others, I do not think that the hidden area of the cover exactly coincides with that part of it which is different in shape and colour from the other part. Rather, I think that continuity obtains between the seen and unseen parts of the lower book's cover. Moving my head to the side, so that my bookstand hides more and more of the monitor screen from me, I do not think that the bookstand eats into the monitor screen, as it were, rather than that the occluded area of the screen continues to exist unchanged. Shouting and waving to a speck in the sky, I do not initially describe it as such, and then as a bird-shape, and then as a bird, and then as my skylark. Rather, I immediately identify it to onlookers as my skylark, the correctness of which becomes increasingly probable as the object approaches and reveals more of its shape and colour, and is confirmed beyond doubt when it perches on my finger. Admiring its curves on the near side, I expect it to be symmetrically rounded. If the far side turns out to be flat, I at least expect what was the near side to still be curved.

Perhaps we could combine a visual and auditory example as follows. Let a trilling sound misdirect me, as before, which I become aware of when I spot the skylark hovering in a different part of the sky. Donning my wingsuit, I chase after it only for it to disappear and re-appear elsewhere, this being repeated every time I try to approach it. Now suppose that on what will turn out to be the last such occasion the skylark disappears, as before, but then changes into a heron, this being the first of its many transformations when I try to make contact. Now continue in this vein but going ever deeper into the unpredictable and unreliable until a limit is reached. If we ask about the nature of this limit, then clearly it concerns language and is reached when the referencing system is mangled beyond the point at which the damage can be described. That the destruction takes this form is indicated even by the surface examples that we gave. A skylark can turn into a heron only if the two species can be referenced, as in the present sentence; but if bird species are constantly and unpredictably interchanging, then the words "skylark" and "heron" will no longer be taxonomically viable.

But is it really true, it might be asked, that nothing is immediately given in perception, in the sense of being epistemically independent? Granted that in looking at an object, I have expectations about the parts of it not yet seen, the correctness of which is not guaranteed, it still is the case, surely, that inference of this kind derives from perception that is immediate by way of being non-inferential, as when I observe those parts of the skylark at present in my field of view. The answer to this is as follows. It is true that they are immediately perceptible in the sense of being visible, the contrast being with parts I cannot see. But it is also true that my directly seeing them is accountable to further such perception, and in ways already explained. Such observations, in other words, are informed by *belief*, just as we believe, other things being equal, that the skylark's curved surface continues on its far side.

This is easily overlooked, because we are presently viewing the near side, which is thereby directly given in the everyday sense, hence the debate as to whether it is directly given in another sense, that which implies that we cannot be mistaken in what we directly observe, provided that we describe it in a way that does not go beyond what is given. I argued in *Beyond Knowledge* that no such description is possible, but in the present instance the issue does not, in any case, arise, since it is clear that any ascribing of spatial depth to an object, in other words any description which implies its physical existence, involves inference and therefore is associated with logically fallible belief.

In the case of seeing the skylark's near side as a curved surface, I have the perceptual expectations by which that impression will either be confirmed or not; and this is to say that, for instance, turning the bird will reveal a curved outline, just as my seeing the side of a bottle as curved will be confirmed if the base of the bottle reveals itself to be curved or round. And in both cases, that of the bird and the bottle, seeing a part of the object as having a particular shape belongs within a system of perceptual beliefs and expectations by which we take the object to retain its identity through change of configuration. What I believe, in short, is that the skylark and the bottle enjoy an objective existence, one that does not depend on being perceived. If, on the other hand, I am in error in all the ways just listed, and if I am increasingly misled in this, then again the phenomenon of "seeing as" will cease to be informative; and this is to say, since all seeing is "seeing as", that visual acquaintance with the world will be on a par with looking down a kaleidoscope while turning it, but without the fascination of changing patterns of reflective symmetry.

If the present line of reasoning is correct, then it demonstrates that phenomenal intentionality is not geared just to the present moment, with nothing of the past and future also being engaged, but that it operates within a system, one in which physical reality does not reveal itself in perceptual acts considered in isolation. Rather, they should be treated as observational processes involving the interplay between the occurrent and the dispositional, the system being such that general physical existence is part of its structure. It is not something that can be called into question, unlike the particular judgements we make about features of the world. This is in stark contrast to Smith's phenomenological approach, together with his thesis that the fact of perceptual illusion transforms the view we should take of the subjectivity of perception. That being the case, further divergencies of reasoning should emerge when we consider his assessment of theories of perception that compete with his own. This is the task to which we now turn.

## 3.5: Perception and Conception

Having rejected in Chapter 2 the dual component theory by which perception comprises sensation and the exercise of concepts, these being separate functions, Smith now considers in Chapter 3 what he refers to as the monistic counterpart to the theory. This is the view that perceptual sensation is intrinsically conceptual, it being distinct in this way from bodily sensations. If I close my eyes and feel with my fingers an object which I thereby recognise as a wire tensioner on a fence post, then this is an example of tactile perception; but if I jump back in pain, realising too late that this is an electric fence, then this is an example of bodily, not perceptual, sensation, despite all the information it conveyed to me in that particular observational context. The theory I outlined earlier, that perception is intrinsically inferential, invites comparison with – or to – the conceptualism which Smith rejects, arguing as he does that concepts are irrelevant to perception. Since he does not deny that they are intimately associated with what it is to perceive, it is clear that the points at issue are subtle, so that the first step should be to tease out their intricacies.

By way of illustration, Smith asks whether one can perceive a typewriter without having the concept of it as a device for performing certain functions. The gist of his argument, If I may take the liberty of using my own examples, is that both a modern computer user and a primitive typist see the same physical object, despite the computer user, if she has led a sheltered life, having no idea what it is for. They would, Smith acknowledges, have different reactions, intentions and so forth in relation to the object, and different uses for it, this being an example of the agreed close link between perception and concepts; but they would see the same object in more or less the same way. I put it like that in order to allow for the possibility, as Smith does, of slight perspectival differences, his point being that this would not be the difference between having perceptually meaningless sensations and perceiving a physical object.

Indeed it would not, but Smith's example proves nothing, leaving open as it does the possibility that the two subjects see the typewriter in the same way because their basic visual concepts are the same; and, too, because the non-basic concept of a typewriter, which only one of them possesses, is not such as to interfere with their mutual seeing of it as a physical object of a certain size and shape. As for the character of these basic concepts, my argument is that perception is intrinsically inferential within a system, where this is to be understood in terms of inference being dispositional as well as occurent, the same there-fore being true of perception – and, of course, of the exercise of concepts.

All this will be explained in detail, my concern for the moment being to establish a reference point for the theories under discussion, insofar as their relative positions can be approximately ascertained. In fact, not even this is strictly necessary, let alone the mapping of subtle points of similarity and difference between the theory in terms of a system and, in the present case, the theories of perception which Smith labels as conceptualism. All that counts, really, is that perception is inferential, this being at variance with his claim that concepts are irrelevant to the essential character of what it is to perceive a physical object.

It should be obvious that inference of the kind in question involves concepts, but imagine, just in case, that I am looking at this canary on my keyboard, that being how I describe it, thereby inferring from the visible to the hidden, or from the present to the future or conditional future. A concise way of expressing this is to say that the reference to canary and keyboard goes beyond the immediately given. This is, however, potentially misleading, it being more accurate to say that the reference goes beyond anything that could conceivably be regarded as being immediately given, except that it takes longer. Even this, however, is liable to misdirect, for the fact is that nothing can be given in the sense of standing alone, a condition which perhaps can be approached within limits, though even this is debatable.

If I speak of the curved yellow visible side of the object, then I imply that this near side is colour fast, as it were. Also, that it has presently hidden aspects, for instance a far side, and that its curved shape, if real, imposes constraints on its appearance from slightly changing perspectives, as does any shape it seems to have. None of this can be squared with the claim that basic perceptions or perceptual judgements are self-contained, with its overtones of incorrigibility, nor does it align itself with the view that concepts are irrelevant to what it is to perceive – or not unless it is beside the point, on such a view, that perception necessarily involves the exercise of memory, recognition, expectation, "perceiving as" and inference. But then, the view in question would be of little interest and need not detain us further.

In fact, Smith distinguishes between what he refers to as high and low conceptualism, the former being the view that perception necessarily involves high-level thinking and conceptualising, naturally associated, one might suppose, with the use of language at the level of human communication. Smith rejects this version of the theory, partly on the grounds that non-human animals are able to perceive, as also that human perception does not necessarily involve sophisticated thought. A non-typist can perceive a typewriter as an object having certain physical characteristics, just as a non-electrician can give a detailed description of an electrical insulator, ignorant of the fact that it has that function. There is nothing here I would wish to reject in itself, but it is worth pointing out that the difference between high and low in this context is one of degree, both of them involving the occurrent and the dispositional, rather than that high concepts involve conscious thinking, thereby distancing themselves from those at a lower level.

If I were to take this further, I would argue that only human beings are capable of philosophy, which necessarily involves the sophisticated use, relative to other species, of language and concepts, such use being intimately associated, as we have seen that Smith himself would agree, with processes of human perception, albeit not as a necessary condition at this higher level. But it *is* a necessary condition at the lower level, that at which perception depends on recognition, expectation, inference and memory, as with the non-typist's perception of a typewriter; and, too, the difference between high and low is one of degree, so that the typist's relatively sophisticated conception of the typewriter he uses is, contrary to Smith's claim, relevant to the analysis of human perception.

What in fact I propose to say is just that perception depends on recognition, expectation and so on, this being a claim which Smith rejects, contending as he does that concepts are irrelevant to perception even at this lower level. In presenting his argument, he targets recognition as a necessary component of perception, to which end he distinguishes between recognising an object and being able to discriminate between it and others. This latter ability, he says, is necessary to perceiving anything at all, but the same is not true of recognition. He maintains that we can perceive a familiar object and have no idea what it is, as in the case of sufferers from agnosia. They fail to recognise such objects as keys and combs in terms of their function, though at the same time they are able to perceive them and to describe their physical features.

How do they explain, though, the difficulty they have in combing their hair with a key or opening the car door with a comb? We are not told, but in any case this is not a counter-example to the claim, for it just is a fact that with visual agnosia some forms of recognitional ability are impaired but not others. This is obvious from the example, for if the sufferer describes a key, let us say, his seeing of it being normal, then he must be able to recognise it as the same object from one moment to the next. This is not just by virtue of phenomenal resemblance but also through changes of perspective and, correspondingly, of appearance, including apparent shape, colour and size. A difficulty here is that recognition and discrimination are closely connected, as with Smith's own example of our being able to distinguish between two colours, or shades of colour, on a particular occasion and yet not be sure, when shown one of them shortly afterwards, which of the two we are seeing again.

This is meant to indicate that we can discriminate without recognition, but it seems to me that the point is lost in the overlap between these abilities, whence it cannot be retrieved. If I place two red balls of different shades in separate bags, and if I am presented with a third ball identical with one of them, except that I do not know which bag to place it in, then in what sense am I able to discriminate between the two shades of colour? Well, might it not be that I have forgotten them? Indeed it might, but this would indicate, unless it is just a momentary lapse, that I cannot make the discrimination, essential to which is the ability to remember what I perceive, this also being essential to perception itself. But now, a manifestation of that ability is recognitional, as when I place the third ball in the right box, and perhaps the fourth, if there is one, and so on.

In a similar vein, and vulnerable to the same kind of criticism, he now argues that the thesis that perception depends on recognition is incoherent, for there must always be a first time that one perceives an object or feature of a particular kind. This is not a strong argument, and I address it only because by so doing I can make a point about what it is to perceive. Suppose I see the colour turquoise for the first time, perhaps in the form of a dragonfly displaying that colour on its body and wings. But now, it is not the disembodied colour that I see but a turquoise-coloured insect, with all that this implies about the operation of recognition, memory, inference and expectation, as explained in this and earlier chapters.

Very well, but let us consider an example in which the perception of physical objects is kept to a minimum, perhaps by way of a dense, turquoise-coloured mist occupying the whole of my visual field, including the area where I would expect to see my hands and the front of my body. Suppose that I was asleep while this magical transformation into a world of pure colour conjured itself into existence, and that I now open my eyes to turquoise heaven, this being my first experience of either the colour or the place. Suppose further that I soon close them again, too much turquoise being known to cause vivid images of coral islands, and that I am now about to open my eyes and find myself immersed in that colour once more. Then I expect to see the same colour, or if not then I am in any case disposed to remember and recognise it; and this is true however short the time I was resting my eyes.

If it is objected that I might *not* be so disposed, then this is perhaps conceivable in the particular case in question, but that is because pure and uniform colour is all that I see. If I now imagine that it starts to resolve itself into physical form symmetric about a centre, which metamorphosises into the turquoise body of a dragonfly, its wings condensing from the mist on each side, then it no longer makes sense, even, to say that I behold these wonders without the aid of recognition, memory, inference and so on. To the contrary, they permeate the perceptual processes by which I register the unfolding of these events, without which the deliverances of perception would be devoid of narrative content and the physical world reduced to sense-datum chaos. And, of course, it is the perception of physical objects, in this case a dragonfly, that perceptual analysis is concerned with, not the experience of turquoise mist as representative of a world of pure colour.

Smith has much more to say that is of analytical interest but we shall not concern ourselves with it, preferring instead to engage directly with his attempted solution to the sceptical problem and his arguments in defence of direct realism.

## 3.6: Smith's Proposed Solution

We shall consider the main part of Smith's anti-sceptical solution, the key to which, he claims, derives from Kant, who maintained that in perception, unlike sensation, one can distinguish phenomenologically between a change of perceptual experience and an experience of change in the physical object or event. This distinction, we are told, connects with what psychologists refer to as perceptual constancy, of which there are different kinds, one of which is position constancy. It obtains when, for instance, I move my eyes while viewing this table, so that my visual experience changes, and yet the table itself does not appear to move.

Again, if I walk up to an object it occupies more of my visual field, and yet, or so it is claimed, it does not look any larger, though it does look nearer: this is an example of what is referred to as size constancy. Smith now considers cases of perspectival relativity for instance that of looking at a penny tilted away from you, so that the usual claim is that it appears elliptical. He disputes this, maintaining as he does that the penny 'looks just the way it is: round and *tilted away from you.*'(p.172) This, he says, is an example of shape constancy. He goes on, 'All such constancies involve a change in visual experience, a change in visual sensation, despite the fact that the object of awareness does not itself appear to change at all. This is because the changes in sensation *themselves have objective significance*: there is a change in how the physical world perceptually appears to us.' (ibid)

Smith now explains why it is that the phenomenological constancies are central to defending direct realism from the illusion argument. Given their existence, he says, it follows that a sensation or sense datum cannot be a perceptual object, for if it were then perceptual constancy would not be possible. He illustrates this point by asking what the sense-datum account would be of the phenomenology of looking at an object as it approaches. The answer, he says, is that it would be said that the sense data of the object increase in size, rather than that the object appears as the same size but drawing nearer, this being an example of size constancy. Thus it is, according to Smith, that sense-datum theory is incompatible with perceptual constancy. He now maintains that the only theory of perception left standing is that of direct realism.

## 3.7: Judgement Day

It is time, I think, to pass judgement on Smith's proposed solution, this to be done by assuming initially, in order to appraise the arguments based on it, that his account of the phenomenology of perceptual constancy is correct, that account then being scrutinised in its turn. Is it really true that sense-datum theory cannot accommodate the notion of perceptual constancy? Certainly, a phenomenalist would deny it, for her thesis is that if, to use the everyday vernacular, she walks her dog in a field and calls to it to come to her, then both it and the field are logical constructions out of sense data, irrespective of whether the dog looks the same size as it runs towards her. Indeed, all those who believe that the idea of a sense datum is coherent, whether phenomenalists or not, could maintain, in the light of that belief, that there is no special difficulty about constancy. They would argue that the increasing size of visual sense data in a temporal sequence may be interpreted as the approach of the object which the sense data represent. Smith, as we know, has hitherto given every sign of treating the theory of sense data as being coherent and perspicuous, the need for detailed semantic explication thereby being obviated.

One would expect, after all, that the concept of a logical construction, given its apparent flexibility, could be persuaded to take account of perceptual constancy; though how this might be done is not our concern. In our earlier criticisms we sought to prevent the notion of a sense datum from gaining any initial traction. But still, if we do not wish to argue ad hominem, then we need to consider Smith's thesis in its own right.

The problem here is that once we allow sense data into the fray, perhaps characterised as perception-dependent entities of some kind, then this in itself makes them very easy enemies attackable on all sides, the noise of the artillery muting any forays in which perceptual constancy is deployed. To see this, we need only consider simple perception such as my looking at this wine bottle, for which purpose we shall grant to Smith the correctness of his thesis about the phenomenally intentional. If I see the near side of the bottle as curved, and curved again when I turn it in my hand, and the base of the bottle as a circular disc, then the notion of a sense datum may be brought into play, though only in order to make a particular point. Thus: I have a visual sense datum of a curved area, and then another, and then a circular sense datum or sense datum of a disc. But nothing connects them, and each obtains only in the moment I experience it.

Nothing counts as different appearances of the same physical object, for there are only momentary sense data. Consider again this keyboard on this table. I have a sense datum, or so we are pretending, of the keyboard and then the table; but I cannot have a sense datum corresponding to the keyboard being on the table, in particular of its partially covering the table. It follows yet again that the whole idea of sense data as perceptual proxies is unable to get a grip. But this conclusion proceeds from the very nature of sense data and depends not at all on any appeal to perceptual constancy. It just is a fact that on Smith's own showing there cannot be sense data if they are understood to be perception-dependent. For just as we would say that they increase in size, not that an object is nearer, so we would say that they cease to exist, not that we no longer perceive the object.

Finally, let us ask whether Smith's phenomenological account should be accepted. Is it really true that when I look at a tilted penny I see it not as elliptical but as round and tilted away from me? Clearly, I may know that it is tilted, but is this given to me in my visual experience of looking at the penny? Part of the problem here, as we have seen, is that it is by no means clear what the notion of an item being given in sense-experience, or immediately given, amounts to. What I suggest is that we bypass the issue via the route of analysing the conditions by which perceptual constancy obtains, as opposed to engaging in a debate whose terms are ill-defined.

# Chapter 4: Perceiving the Senses

Let us begin with a quibble as to the accuracy of describing a tilted penny as looking elliptical. An ellipse is a two-dimensional shape, whereas a tilted penny typically exhibits spatial depth if it is near enough for the relevant features to be discerned. This is, in fact, a point that Smith himself makes, apart from the proximity condition, and it connects with a common criticism of visual sense data conceived of as two-dimensional coloured shapes. It is a valid criticism, though this does not impede Smith from taking sense data seriously. Our present concern, however, is with his claim that a coin may look round and tilted, which does not follow from its not looking elliptical, nor from its appearing to exhibit spatial depth.

Since an obstacle to clear thinking here is that most tilted coins are recognised as coins, and thereby known to be round, or seen to be round, before being tilted, let it be supposed that I gaze at previously unseen objects fixed on a stand in such a way as to be rotatable, and that I cannot alter my present visual perspective on them, perhaps because my head is in a vice. Let the objects be tilted coins, one of them appearing edge-on, and consider Smith's claim that I see them as both round and tilted, this being immediately given, so that it owes nothing to inference or judgement. On the principle that we cannot see what does not exist, astronomers and infatuates excepted, or is invisible from a given perspective, Smith's claim has to be wrong, for the appearance of these objects is consistent with an unlimited range of non-circular shapes, as is most obvious from consideration of the object seen edge-on.

Clearly, the only restriction on shape, if the object is in fact a coin, coins being flat, derives from the condition that no part of the rest of the object should be visible when the object is seen edge-on, from which perspective it appears either as a curved edge or, in projected outline, as a very narrow rectangle. It could, for instance, be an oval object with a milled edge, a ring or segment of a ring, an object with a flat edge made to look curved, and so on. This claim about unlimited morphological possibilities remains true, though not so strikingly, if the object is rotated from full-face but stops short of being presented edge-on.

In fact, Smith's visual constancy thesis as it stands is mistaken; for if, for instance, I glimpse an approaching object so distant as to be barely visible, on the straight path which runs ahead of me through fields of summer corn to the next hamlet, and if it resolves itself eventually into my sweet love come courting, then in what way does the original faraway speck present itself as the same size as this fair maid who now greets me? One might as well maintain that they are seen as having the same shape. Clearly, a qualification as to proximity and visible detail is needed, a question arising as to how many other conditions would have to be fulfilled.

This is all so conspicuously true that one wonders how it could ever be denied: and, indeed, it is no surprise when Smith moderates, or seems to moderate, his thesis by making concessions to common sense. That thesis, he now acknowledges, should not be taken to extremes: 'When I walk up to an unchanging object while looking at it, there is *some* sense in which something grows in extensity.'(p.183) This is, he says, a necessary condition of constancy, for if two objects look the same size and one looks nearer, then it must have greater extensity. In other words, it must occupy a greater part of one's visual field. This is not, however, enough to establish the thesis, not even in a weaker form, for of two objects one can take up more of one's visual field without appearing the same size as the other, as with the previous counter-example of watching someone approach along a path. Besides, Smith has already stated, as part of his thesis, that perceptual constancy involves changes in sense-experience, so that all that his present qualification amounts to is that such changes may disguise the fact of constancy, as with an object looming larger in one's visual field.

We have now criticised Smith's proposed solution, insofar as it relates to sense-datum theory, on two fronts: the visual and the auditory. Also, we have challenged his account of perceptual constancy as it applies to vision, so that we are left with its application to audition. I argued just now that the notion of an auditory sense datum seems even more problematic than that of a visual sense datum, because visual perception seems transparent to its object, whereas the auditory kind does not, even though we speak of "hearing as" just as we speak of "seeing as", this latter lending itself even more to confusion about the nature of sense data, or at least to a different kind of confusion.

My present point is that even if sense data are set aside, Smith's account not only of visual but also of auditory constancy is confused. If I see a bull as getting nearer, not bigger, then in order to appreciate that this is not immediately given, I have to reflect on the phenomenology involved and the role of intentionality. But if, without seeing the bull, I hear it as getting nearer, not louder, then it is evident that inference is involved, for instance that I infer to the presence of a bull as the source of the sound. If this is not obvious, then perhaps the mistake one makes is to equate inference with conscious reasoning, its dispositional character being overlooked.

I think that enough has been said to expose the failure of Smith's proposed solution to the illusion problem, the main thrust of which lacks penetrative power. There is an irony here in the fact that his proposal, phenomenological in character, concerns an aspect of perception, that of perceptual constancy, which so obviously involves inference and belongs within a system. He rejects the possibility that, as he puts it, such constancy consists in a judgement one makes, perhaps on the basis of past experience, in response to what one is immediately aware of. This, although rejected, seems to me to be nearer the truth, except that it would have to be so heavily qualified that the resulting account, in the context of a theory of perception in terms of a system, would bear little resemblance to it. Since that theory has already been sketched out in the present critique of Smith's analysis of perception, I now suggest that we fill in the details with regard to the theory's application to the constancy phenomenon, consideration of which can then be extended to cover the general question of the relations between perceptual content and conditions.

Let us begin with perceptual constancy depending on a range of circumstances which determine whether an object is perceived as bigger than another, or than its earlier self, or nearer, or both at the same time or in succession. Suppose I notice two specks in the sky, one of them seemingly motionless, the other occupying an increasing area of my visual field, in other words, *pace* Smith, looking bigger. Eventually I am able to make out enough detail, or pick up enough cues, to recognise it as a balloon. Given that it looks bigger, should I say that it looks nearer than the other, or than its earlier self?

Well, it depends on this and that, hence the conditionality referred to just now. A general principle, as here instantiated, is that an object increasing in apparent size appears closer to the observer; but then, perhaps it *is* increasing in size. Indeed, the principle has to be hedged about with many qualifications, owing to the complexity of the subject matter of the psychology of perception, for instance with regard to the interrelationship of factors which determines one's perception of three-dimensional objects.

Suppose, then, that the skylark perched on my finger takes off to investigate the balloon, my view after a minute or two being of the balloon occluding the skylark, which disappears behind it and then re-appears from its other side, only to occlude in its turn, albeit only partially, a flock of crows which I noticed passing overhead a few minutes before. Such a sequence of events, given its timing, is informative as to the distance of the balloon relative to myself and other objects. The cues involved, according to the experts, are processed for the most part below the level of the conscious perception which is partly determined by them.

Our concern, however, is not with pre-conscious perceptual causation, which I mention only to make the point that our concern is not with it, but with the phenomenology of perceptual constancy philosophically considered, and with its place within a system. If we suppose that the balloon looks bigger, and that it looks nearer, hence my being able to discern more detail, then "bigger" and "nearer" are relational terms, thereby implying a comparison between objects which may or may not be co-present. If they are, as with the balloon compared with the other object, if it still appears as a speck in the sky, or if they are not, as with the balloon as it is now and as it was earlier, then the salient point is that this is not a fundamental difference. If the balloon and the speck are both in my field of view, so that I focus on the one while keeping the other in sight, then this differs only in degree from viewing them separately in different parts of the sky; and this in its turn differs in the same way from one of them, say the speck, having disappeared, so that it is present only in memory when I look at the other.

This all follows quite naturally from the notion of a system and its emphasis on interrelations and the crucial role of inference, expectation, memory and so on, not only in relating different perceptual objects but also in the perceiving of a single event regarded as a temporal process in its own right. The point is not that an object cannot of itself look bigger or nearer, on the grounds that these are phenomena involving relations between different objects perceived; rather, the point is that an object can indeed look nearer, let us say, than it did before, but that inference and relationality are fundamental to the phenomenology involved. This is opposed to the view that an object's appearance is immediately given, so that it is linked to other objects, or to the perception of them, or of itself at other times. Such a link is not conceptual but only contingent, for instance in ways that are the subject matter of the science of perception. My point, as always, is that nothing in perception is immediately given, where this includes distance and size, as also the physical identity on which they depend. This latter, however, connects with shape constancy, to which we now return.

To begin with, many of our findings about size constancy also apply to shape, as in the example of a stand supporting a rotatable coin. Smith would claim that we see it as tilted and round through change of perspective, its shape constancy being immediately given, even in the extreme case of the coin being viewed edge-on. In rejecting that claim, I pointed out that the parts of the object not visible from a particular point of view could take any form consistent with its present appearance. The way in which it appears edge-on is not such as to exclude its being oval, for instance, as opposed to round; therefore, I argued, its roundness could not be immediately given. We should have to say, after all, that viewed face-on, its roundness was *more* immediately given.

None of this is to deny that perceptual consciousness and phenomenal character are of the essence of what it is to perceive; nor that one may speak of what is given in perception, as with referring to the contents of one's visual or other sense-field. What is needed, then, is to distinguish between the perceptually and the immediately given, such that the concept of the former, but not the latter, has legitimate application.

To that end, let us return to the example of the coin on a stand, imagining, as before, that it is viewed edge-on. Suppose this time that my companion, whom I forgot to mention earlier, is in exile from a steeply inclined land where round coins have been replaced, on safety grounds, by oval ones, owing to the high incidence of injuries caused by coins rolling out of control. My companion, like myself, knows nothing about this present object, apart from what he can see of it, which is the same as I can see of it.

That being the case, we should be able to describe it in the same way, provided that we are strict in matching description to object, or object-part. We could not, for example, speak of the object-part as having a milled edge, since this is to refer to a manufacturing process or its end product. Suppose we agree that we are looking at an object-part with a curved edge, rectilinear in projected outline, all from the particular perspective that we share. But now, this would seem to be not strict enough, for I have argued that nothing is immediately given, or not if this is to imply that ostensive reference may be infallible or incorrigible. In the present case, for instance, it might be that what seems to be the curved edge of an object-part is really a disguised flat edge.

The general point here, as already made, is that the attribution of spatial depth belongs within a system, for instance that it goes beyond the perceptual snapshot, as it were, and constrains adjacent perspectives. If an object is correctly seen as curved, then that is how it will be seen, and not as a flat edge, if viewed from a slightly different angle. Thus it is that the possibility of perceptual or observational confirmation is brought into play, together with the implied perceptual beliefs.

If we now ask what it is that perception being informed by belief consists in, and if we return to the coin example, then we may suppose, as before, that my companion and I are looking at the object edge-on, except that this time it has dawned on both of us that the object is a coin. For my companion, however, coins are oval, whereas for me they are round. What difference, if any, could this make to the actual experience of looking at the coin, this being such as to reflect the difference in belief as to the shape it would display if seen face-on? Seeking an answer, it may be recalled that a similar question was asked about belief and understanding in general, this being the topic of an earlier chapter. My thesis was that these and other forms of the intentional are occurrent within a dispositional framework. If this is correct, then one may speak of what one believes at a particular moment, given that the intentionality of the present always goes beyond it. the same being true of the way in which perceiving an object unfolds.

Applying all this to the case under discussion, the question to be asked, about my companion and myself, concerns the different ways in which we perceive the coin from one moment to the next. This is to focus on perception as a process which involves the confluence of dispositional and occurent in the same perceptual stream. If, for instance, the coin starts to turn, so that its face comes increasingly into view, then my seeing it as round is now a continuous process of visual expectations confirmed, and others following on, these also confirmed, the flow of expectation and confirmation merging smoothly into the observational experience by which the face of the coin is revealed. What my companion finds, however, is that perceptual obstacles confront his expectations, the result being disconfirmation as the flow of visual consciousness breaks against the immovable reality of the coin being round, not oval. It may then re-form and run smoothly, expectation and "perceiving as" merging together as gradually the now expected roundness of the coin takes shape.

## 4.1: Perceptual Variability

This is a point worth making, but what I now propose is to go deeper into the issue, noting first that it arises only if the possibility of an object maintaining its physical identity is presupposed. If the issue is that of whether anything fundamental is involved in what is given in perception as opposed to inferred, this being addressed by consideration of the particular case of observing an object-part, putatively belonging to a coin, then the stability and physical identity of such objects moment by moment is presupposed as a property of the framework in which the issue is discussed. But what we perceive of objects, for instance what we see of them, is characterised not by uniformity, as a simplistic notion of identity might suggest, but by *variability*, the appearance of an object depending on a host of factors, such that its physical identity transcends them, there being a level at which transcendence in this respect is irreducible.

At another level, however, we may speak of the inferential nature of perception, whereby the different facets of an object are linked together by relations of memory and expectation, these being realised in observational processes or idling, as it were, in the form of dispositions. Thus, we may examine an unfamiliar object, perhaps a coin if normally we only use plastic, in order to acquaint ourselves with its shape. The physical identity of the coin transcends its different appearances when viewed edge-on, or tilted, or full-face, or close up, or at arm's length, and so on, the same applying to the way in which the deliverances of our other senses inform our conception of the coin. But now, if perceptual inference operating over variability of sense-content with respect to physical identity is a central feature of perception, then the question of what exactly is given becomes peripheral, its interest having been exhausted.

It is time to move on, my aim in this final section being twofold: to directly confront the illusion argument and to dispel any reservations one might have about whether a system-based account of perception can avoid the charge of being tantamount to indirect realism. According to the illusion argument, the possibility of illusory perception lends itself to scepticism in the form of anti-realism. This is a narrower basis for scepticism than that which supports the views of many who reject the theory of direct realism. In the opening pages of this chapter, indeed, I listed several aspects of perception which the sceptic finds problematic, and these include the phenomenon of perspectival relativity, which, unlike illusion regarded as perceptually deviant, is of the very essence of what it is to perceive the physical world.

For Smith, as we have seen, this phenomenon, or that of the perceptual constancy which transcends it, may be supportive of direct realism if treated in a certain way. For A.J.Ayer, on the other hand, variability of appearance threatens what he refers to as naive realism. If an object which we take to persist over time, the usual example being one which changes very slowly, such as a pebble, is known to us only by its appearances, which vary according to conditions, then in what sense, he asks, does it preserve its physical identity? (1973a, p.78). How, in other words, are we to distinguish between the object and the range of appearances by which it manifests itself to the perceiver?

Ayer detects a difficulty here, and it is one which obliges him, he thinks, to treat appearances as entities in their own right. This is a pivotal point, as we know from previous consideration of sense data and sensible or sensory qualities. And, as before, the turning of a theory of perception towards perceptual proxies or entities trapped between the physical and the mental needs to be resisted, to which end it should be noted that nothing in a system-based account points in that direction. If it did, then I would be guilty of the incoherent reasoning I have charged the sense-datum theorists with. Far from that being the case, I have argued that taking the deliverances of the senses in general to reveal an objectively existing physical world is intrinsic to perception. When, for instance, I think I am looking at a coin, my view of which is necessarily partial, then I register its particular appearance as that which an *object-part* presents to me, the object located within independently existent physical surroundings.

## 4.2: Illusion as Argument

That, at any rate, is what I have tried to show, albeit by opposing the argument from illusion, not this wider sceptical approach. Perhaps we should scrutinise this latter, especially if it can also be shown, as I think it can, that a sceptical reading of the possibility of illusion extends naturally to scepticism based on the phenomenon of perspectival relativity. For this to be shown, consider what it is for a straw, or what seems to be a straw, to be held above a fish tank, its submerged part looking bent. If I have no prior knowledge of the shape of the straw, then various morphological possibilities present themselves. Perhaps what I see is a straight straw looking bent in water, or a bent straw, the bend at the water line, the submerged part looking more or less bent than it really is, the bend being original to the straw or brought about by immersion; or, another possibility: a bent straw undistorted in the way it looks, the "water" actually being a clear liquid in which the apparent shape of an object is its real shape.

These are the possibilities it is reasonable to consider, an unlimited number of others, their range circumscribed only by the limits of one's imagination, being left out of account because one attaches no weight to them. If it is now asked what the straw's real shape might be, there are various methods of ascertaining this, the point being that they all involve further observation in which inferential processes of perception are played out. That the straw is straight, its looking bent being an illusion, is just one possibility, and on the same inferential level as the others. The salient feature is just that its appearance in water, albeit only when first encountered, is liable to mislead the observer, for in all other everyday circumstances further observation will reveal that the straw *is* bent.

There is, then, a difference, but it is hidden in the folds of the fundamental similarity between veridical and illusory perception, which operate within a system in which perceptual processes are intrinsically inferential. If a stick looks bent in water, the bend may be real or illusory, the stick's appearance being consistent with both. If the view of the part above water from a particular angle is of straight, parallel sides defining an apparent curved surface, then the object-part, although it looks curved, may in fact be flat. In any case the object, its far side hidden from view, may be any shape consistent with its present appearance; and the notion of consistency in this connection itself has content only within a system. If the differences in question are superficial, as I suggest, then this is to say that perceptual scepticism based exclusively on the fact or possibility of illusion is illicitly restricted.

That the superficiality really does obtain is indicated by what seem to be demarcation difficulties with the notion of perceptual illusion. Are mirror reflections illusory? Or the apparent narrowing of straight railways lines, as if converging at infinity, despite the train not stopping there.? What of objects seen at a distance? The Neolithic tumuli I can see from my garden on the skyline of a far-away hill look two-dimensional, in keeping with their being, say, very large semi-circular boards: is this an illusion? I do not have to believe that they are boards standing up, after all, in order for my perception of them to be illusory.

And, too, it is worth pointing out that the central role of inference in perception creates another levelling effect: that between illusion and hallucination, which some philosophers, Smith in particular, treat quite separately in their work on perceptual scepticism. But the bent part of a stick in water, if illusory, has no more substance than these tiny kangaroos on my keyboard; and neither do apparently converging railway lines, or what seems to be a semi-circular featureless shape on a hill. One might argue that with hallucination nothing at all exists of the hallucinatory object, but this does not seem to be of great significance; and in any case nothing at all exists of the bent part of the stick, the same being true, arguably, of the semi-circular figure and the converging rails.

## 4.3: Direct Realism

What we are left with is the common-sense theory from which we started, that of direct realism, which I propose to consider in the context of a system. The reason is partly that it should then be easy to dispose of the sceptic's arguments, those which underpin the problem of perception, to which sense-data theory may be seen as an attempt to provide a sceptical solution. To begin with, we conceive of the external world as enjoying an objective existence independently of our perceiving it. If I take my eyes off this table, I know that it continues in its usual state, basically just vegetating in a wooden kind of way, without any help from me. By way of justifying my claim to know, I could adduce the astonishing coincidence of the table ceasing to exist at the exact moment I looked away, or the fact that the other people seated around it would surely have noticed. The point about this or any other way of justifying my claim is that it presupposes the general perceptually independent existence of physical objects; and in particular of this room and its occupants, which I cannot continually perceive, and of my eyes, which I mostly never see. This, then, is part of what is included in the notion of a system.

What that notion also accommodates is the fact that perceptual appearance varies according to conditions. The point here is that when we identify an object we are fully aware of such facts as that its visual appearance from one moment to the next depends on perspective, illumination, ocular conditions and so on. Since direct realism must be taken to be correct, its rivals having been eliminated, the facts of perceptual variation and conditionality cannot be legitimately exploited by the sceptic. We must accept what cannot be denied, and one way for the sceptic in us to find a pillow for unquiet thought is to fall back on the concept of irreducibility. Suppose, then, that I examine an everyday object, say a length of wood of square cross-section, which I hold in my hand. I can position it in such a way as to directly see only the coloured square of its base; but if I tilt it, so that the base and a side or two sides are visible, then the object is exhibited directly as having spatial depth, this being the way in which we see the world, the point being that it cannot be reduced to the seeing of two-dimensional coloured shapes.

Not only that but it is intrinsic to seeing spatial depth in this way that the experience is a vehicle for the belief that the object is three-dimensional and has the shape it seems to have, this being the default position by which exceptions to the rule are framed, as with mistaking a cardboard cut-out for the object it represents. Again, then, we discover a system at work; and, too, if the notion of irreducibility is brought back into play, for instance with regard to the piece of wood, and if a question arises as to what exactly it is in this case that manifests or causes the given visual appearances, changing as they do according to the laws governing perspective, illumination and so on, then the only answer is that it is a piece of wood of a certain size, shape and colour. The description of an object as being three-dimensional is irreducible, as is our understanding of it.

Having met the challenge of the sceptic, let us ask whether the difficulties to which he draws attention, if suitably neutralised, lend themselves to conceptual analysis, their treatment brought into line with direct realism. Given that the appearance of an object exhibits variation, are there hidden criteria by which we determine its real size, shape and colour? According to Ayer, such criteria are linked to standard conditions of observation, and we may ask whether it is possible to specify those conditions. Again, a question arises as to the causal connection between objects and our perception of them, as with this table playing a part in the causal processes by which I see it. Such questions are non-sceptical, for they take for granted the objective reality of the external world.

Finally, and by way of completing the circle, I suggest that we develop the remarks in the first paragraph about our understanding of perception. It has been argued in these chapters that perceptual judgement belongs within a system; for instance, if one refuses to believe that what seems to be a real object really exists, then this is possible only within a perceptual scheme in which the evidence of our senses is in general taken to be veridical. But the system in question is all-encompassing, for induction and knowledge of the past enter into perceptual judgement. If I say that this is a table, I imply that the parts I cannot presently see will have the size, shape, spatial relations and colour appropriate to this being a table, or one that comes under a particular description. But this itself is to imply that I can correctly remember what I now observe of the table.

A particular inductive inference, however, can be justified, confirmed or denied only if others are taken to be correct, the same applying to particular memories. Thus, memory and induction belong within the same system as the perceptual judgements which depend on them. But it can be shown that sceptical arguments about induction or knowledge of the past are self-refuting. It follows, with regard to perception, memory and induction that doubt can be expressed in particular cases only if others are held steady. If general scepticism is ruled out, then the system must be self-justifying — or, perhaps better, such that the question of justification arises only internally and in particular cases.

## 4.4: Perception and its Imperatives

In this last section I shall argue that perceptual processes bridge the gap between logic and fact. If I look at this unfamiliar hat, and if I know only that it is made of uniformly thick material, then immediately I conclude, given its external shape, that it is concave on the inside. But also, that the owner's head does not end where the brim of the hat begins—on the contrary, it fits inside the hat. If I twirl the hat anti-clockwise, the owner having a very flexible neck, then each view of the hat from changing perspectives has to jigsaw into place; and a shift to clockwise twirling, the subject's cries being heeded, would be ruled by strict constraints on the reverse order of viewing. Here, too, fact and logic begin to lean towards each other, like headstones, as always where necessary conditions are involved.

But is it not the case, one might ask, that perceptual experience informs the present example? For instance, it is because of my past observations of the way that a hat is worn that I know empirically that it fits over the subject's head, not just on it. No doubt that is part of the explanation, another part being given in the previous paragraph; but it is also true that an observation is an interpretation, in the present case that we do not register the upper part of the subject's head as dematerialising on contact with the hat—rather, we see the hat being pulled down over the head, which remains intact, the upper part hidden from view. If we now try to imagine the bizarre interpretation taking epistemic precedence over the familiar one, then there is nothing in the particular case of a hat and a head that might preclude extension to the general case.

But the general case would be the epitome of chaos; for the principle at work would be as follows: that an object-part dematerialises when contiguous with another object-part or object. For then the unseen part of the hat would dematerialise when pulled over the head, which itself would follow suit, with basically only the face, or the visible part of it, still standing. And then, of course, the hat would fall off, with more of it disappearing where it touches the ground, except that the part of the ground in contact with… and so on. Perception is constrained in different ways, the significance of which will depend on the reality behind the separation of fact and logic, one of our over-arching aims being to mediate between them with a view to reconciliation. And similarly in the case of probability theory and practice, to which we now turn.

# Chapter 5: Probability and its Problems

My plan for this and the following chapters, to which I shall add various details as we go along, is to continue to chart the deeper currents of the human intellect, by which I imply that carpet mites, at least of the aquatic variety, will be left to their own devices in the shallows of instinct and conditioned response. The thesis I have presented is that reasoning about the world belongs within a system, one that is characterised by connectedness and conditionality. Such a notion challenges one's preconceptions about mathematical and empirical reasoning having their own ports of call and ships of the line. Part of the problem, as we shall see, is that the empiricist view is that so-called applied mathematics itself separates out, under analysis, into pure and applied, this latter being inferential but not deductive. As for the former, there are those, including A.J.Ayer, who would argue that pure mathematics is analytic, the problem then shifting to that of what this means.[1]

In probability theory, too, there are different views as to its classificatory status, with logical probability, for instance, distinguished from other kinds, the number and character of which will depend upon the individual theorist or school of thought. We shall ask whether all this labelling activity muddies the waters, our thesis being that there is only the one probability ocean, not a proliferation of seas.

## 5.1: Types of Probability

What I now propose is that we discuss the issues, pausing only when we have said enough, given the complexity of the subject matter, to be able to return to the question of what we hope to achieve. Perhaps we should begin with commentators varying in what they take to be the main types of probability, in which case Ayer's distinction between *a priori* and statistical probability is not without interest, a third class, as he calls it, being that of judgements of credibility. (1972) *A priori* probability, he says, relates to the calculus of chances, for instance as it enters into the throw of a die or toss of a coin, this latter perhaps in the form of a one in eight probability of a fair coin landing heads thrice in succession. Immediately, however, several hands are raised, mainly in connection with coins or dice being true or fair. Is this to imply that in a series of trials the six faces of each die would have the same relative frequency?

But relative frequency, or so I shall argue in detail, is itself a probability concept, the application of which depends on statistical methods of frequency testing, the use of which belongs to the second kind of probability according to Ayer's classification. Again, if "true" implies relative frequency, then how does it connect with the *a priori*? If it does not, then a puzzle arises as to what could be meant, but in any case it seems clear from what he goes on to say that his concern is with classical probability, the proponents of which he criticises for conflating logical possibility with empirical frequency. This brings the principle of indifference into play, according to which the six faces of a die are equipossible, there being nothing to choose between them, and therefore equiprobable. But suppose that the die is repeatedly thrown, the outcomes recorded; then there may be a disparity, such that the die is no longer taken to be fair, given the divergent frequency findings.

So it is that these distinguishable classes of probability, if Ayer is correct, in fact give every impression of being different aspects of the same probability system. That leaves judgements of credibility, on Ayer's showing, in other words the belief that an event is likely to happen, or more likely than another with which it may be compared, as referred to a moment ago. But now, it is characteristic of the ascribing of probability values, irrespective of one's classificatory scheme, that the events to which they apply are believed to be likely or unlikely to occur. If I invite you to toss two coins, using your own if you wish, and to bet against me that they will land two heads as opposed to a head and a tail, and if the odds are fifty-fifty for a minimum stake of £10 a time for each of a hundred bets, neither of us having much else to do, then one event that I think likely to occur is that you will lose a lot of money as the price you pay for not being street-smart.

I have said enough, I trust, to suggest that we are dealing with different aspects of a single system, the possibility of which is worth investigating, as are the implications if the fact is found. I shall now give a more detailed account of my plan, which is to scrutinise the main probability theories via a system-based approach. Using critical analysis as part of that approach, for instance in the case of the frequency theory, it seems to me that our discussion of it will reveal the role that frequency actually plays in terms of connections and conditions. But also, it will be shown that relative frequency in a formal probability context is a theoretical construct, so that it is mathematical as well as empirical—or, better, it draws critical attention to the distinction itself. It should, indeed, be possible to exhibit the empirical as being mathematically constrained, and the probability calculus, with its apparent dependence on mathematics, as being in thrall to the empirical. To that end, I adduce such facts as that although the concept of significance levels is in part mathematical, this latter does not determine the choice of cut-off point, which partly for historical reasons is usually set at 5%.

But surely, it might be said, the problems of probability, confronted by philosophers and acknowledged by practitioners, in particular by statisticians, and in the public domain by frequently incorrect psephologists, cannot be conjured away by analysis. They owe nothing to argumentative legerdemain and everything to … but to what exactly? To their folk origins in the everyday irrational assessment of risk? It is arguable, I suppose, that our Palaeolithic forebears, who we may safely assume lived long enough to procreate, had not only to run fast but to think quick and decide in the blink of an eye. Our non-ancestors, on the other hand, were perhaps the ones who inscribed on pieces of bark their probability insights, pausing only to gaze into the middle distance, the near distance being where the lions were.

This, as I said, is arguably correct, and one could go further, and on safer ground; for it is a well-attested fact that modern humans can be irrational indeed in the probability judgements that they make.[2] Interestingly, these include errors that arise from insufficient alertness to the problematic use of prior probabilities, a charge that the critics of Bayesianism, or Bayesian excess, level at its proponents. But best, perhaps, not to suspect atavism, for irrational belief arising out of ignorance is one thing and informed philosophical disagreement is quite another.

The fact is, in any case, that I claim to be able to resolve such disagreement insofar as this is possible, the method already indicated, and that I can easily fit another arrow to my bow, just in case domestic cats are not usually that big. Consider, then, the problem of reference classes, and in connection with the paradox of Petersen the Swede, which runs as follows. Petersen is a Swede and most Swedes are Protestants; but Petersen makes an annual pilgrimage, on the face of it, to Lourdes, and most such pilgrims are Catholics.[3] What, then, are we to say about the probability that Petersen is among these latter?

One answer is that further information is needed, in particular about the proportion of Swedish pilgrims who are Catholic. The lesson here would be that theorists need to acknowledge that probability evidence may be incomplete, in response to which they should seek out further data—in preference, that is, to choosing or switching to a more forgiving method, perhaps Bayesian, on the grounds that any evidence, however skeletal, provides a structure for the probability calculus to flesh out. This, in my view, is initially what should be said: not that Bayesian Frankensteins must desist from creating monsters of probability mathematics out of a few scraps of data as DNA, this being too strong a criticism, but that they should cease to posit priors merely in order to bring their methods of inference to bear—unless, that is, they can justify that practice.

There is, in other words, an issue to be resolved. Similarly, one may target the excessive use of significance levels to boost the importance of particular findings, for instance in order to elevate them as being worthy of publication in this or that research journal. These are instances of what may be referred to, at the level of reflection upon practice, as internal criticisms among practitioners about theory-tinged methodological differences. They are relative to what may seem to be more serious issues, in the present case concerning reference classes, the problem of which broadens out into that of the underdetermination of theory—or belief—by evidence.

These wider ripples, when rival methods make a splash, become waves at the level of philosophical meta-theory, where this is to imply a division between decks that is instructive in some ways but not in others. Underdetermination has been mentioned, and in connection with more data needing to be accrued; but we have to be careful about letting this requirement have its head, lest in the present case it gallop overboard. From the fact that the proportion of Swedish visitors to Lourdes who are not Catholic is not known but ought to be, it follows not in the slightest that all such questions need to be answered, otherwise none could be asked. Should we, having ascertained that proportion, now make further enquiries, perhaps into the relevant statistics of age, Petersen being in his forties? Or of gender, Petersen being a man? And occupation, Petersen being a travelling salesman? But now we have further questions, the process never-ending, for if Petersen is a peripatetic seller of goods then these may include rosaries, clerical collars and other ecclesiastical ware, which would invest his visits to Lourdes with commercial intent. The implication here is that the problem of underdetermination needs to be placed in context.

Since the present chapter and the next two are devoted to probability issues in philosophy, I should perhaps issue an alert as to the mathematics involved. A basic grasp of the probability calculus would prove useful in this and the next chapter, but the third chapter concerns Bayesian method and is in any case more technical, especially when continuous distributions are discussed in relation to the sampling problem. That said, much of the mathematics, entering as it does into examples of the main probability methods, is in support of a thesis that is also expressed non-mathematically, for it concerns the key epistemic role played by underdetermination in the probability sub-system. The problem is that of justifying the inference from sample to population or proportion, my treatment of which will be comprehensible, I trust, even to those who are not familiar with probability theory.

## 5.2: The Role of Frequency

If we begin with some general observations about frequency, Hume would say that in its probability applications it is inductive in character; therefore, the appeal to probability theory in defence of induction involves a circularity. Keynes, on the other hand, is of the view that it has the evidential force of partial entailment. Bayesian inference theorists, if consulted, would use their methods to match a probability value to the relative frequency data, this latter in the form of a sequence of heads and tails if a coin was tossed. What this indicates is that probability theory, of whatever flavour, must accommodate relative frequency in one way or another; and I shall now try to show, for the attention of empiricists, that it thereby acquires a technical sense that goes beyond the everyday empirical into mathematics.

Suppose that we conduct a coin-tossing experiment in order to ascertain whether a particular coin is biased, the resulting sequence being subjected to statistical analysis according to our preferred method. If the estimate arrived at is that $P(h) = \frac{1}{3}$, where "$h$" = "heads", then this is a formal interpretation of the sequence, which is to say that the distribution of heads and tails is taken to conform to the requirements of independence and randomness and yields the proposition $P(h) = \frac{1}{3}$, all of which involves the probability calculus. Otherwise, and with regard to numerical values, the probability of heads would be taken to be a third only if this was exactly their proportion, in which case it would not be a probability estimate at all but simply a precise measure of such proportion in a finite sequence, one that would change at the next toss of the coin. Finite, that is, because its expression as an infinite sequence limit would be mathematically technical. Its predictive utility, if it had one, would derive not from abstract probability theory but from inductive extrapolation.

Hume, as we know, would compare them and see no difference. Again, consider randomness in particular as a condition, the lack of which would mean that the probability of heads would be taken to be a third even if, quite astonishingly, all the heads in the sequence came first, followed by twice as many tails. If we are correct about these conditions, then to say that $P(h) = \frac{1}{3}$ in a formal probability context is to imply that the sequence of heads and tails exhibits appropriate probabilistic frequency characteristics and that this will continue if the coin is tossed again.

Less formally, which is to say in everyday life, what one understands of the sequence may be more pragmatic. It may be obvious, for instance to a bookie who examines the sequence and wishes to offer odds on heads or tails, that the incidence of heads is about a third; also, that the arrangement of heads and tails is random in the practical sense that it offers no clue, apart from that proportion, as to the outcome of the next toss of the coin. Quite possibly, then, she will offer odds of two to one or skew them to her own advantage.

Having countered the empiricist approach to relative frequency, let us now enquire into its connection with proportion, and more generally with the notion of numerical probability. If a bag contains three black balls and two white, then $P(black) = 0.6$ if it is assumed that each ball is as likely to be drawn as any other. And now suppose a series of trials in each of which a ball is drawn and its colour noted, the colour sequence at the close of the experiment being subjected to statistical analysis, as already explained. If, other things being equal, the resulting relative frequency value deviates beyond acceptable limits from the expected three-fifths, perhaps when maximum likelihoods are ascertained, or if it does not seem to converge to that limit when continued indefinitely, then the original assumption may be placed under scrutiny. This indicates that a truth-conditional connection obtains between proportion and frequency, at least in those cases in which a clear sense may be attached to repetition of instances treated as trials in a statistical experiment. Our difficulty, as we shall see, is that of analysing the connection, the details of which would seem to depend on the particular circumstances; but there is much to enjoy in making the attempt.

Not only is frequency always a factor in any survey of probability concepts, but I shall now argue that very often it flies under the radar, at which level one fails to distinguish between the objective relative frequency of a feature or event and the success rate of one's guesses in relation to it. In a football match in which the toss of a coin decides which team starts the game, the referee need not ensure that the coin is a fair coin, provided that the two captains know nothing of its bias, and in fact he need not toss the coin as opposed to placing the ball over it and inviting them to guess heads or tails. Indeed, it would make no difference if the coin was double-headed or double-tailed, despite the losing captain's outraged protest to the contrary if she became aware of its "unfairness".

## 5.3: Keynes and Logical Probability

J.M.Keynes, mentioned previously but now given our full attention, is accorded that honour as the author of *A Treatise on Probability* (1973), which he wrote as a young man. There has been, of late, a resurgence of interest in his work, but it mainly focusses on his theory of economics, which despite its impact on the wider world need not detain us. His theory of probability, on the other hand, is directly relevant. He is of the view that probability is a logical relation between evidence, or known evidence, and conclusion, such that 'it is without significance to call a proposition probable unless we specify the knowledge to which we are relating it' (4). Despite what this may seem to imply, Keynes denies that his theory is subjective: 'A proposition is not probable because we think it so. When once the facts are given which determine our knowledge, what is probable or improbable in these circumstances has been fixed objectively, and is independent of our opinion.' (4)

Not only has it been fixed objectively but also, since probability is a logical relation between evidence and conclusion, it follows that the effect of new evidence is to change but not to invalidate the old conclusion. Finally, Keynes' principle of indifference has a part to play, the essence of which is that equipossible alternatives are equiprobable.

There is much here that is debatable once elucidated, but we shall have to be selective. One corollary, for Keynes, is that the notion of probabilistic independence becomes that of independence for knowledge, as he refers to it, in line with probability being relative to known evidence. This leads him into some tight corners, for instance when he writes about coin tossing (187). He seems to assume that the usual notion of independent events concerns the absence of a causal relation between them, as opposed to their being epistemically independent. He then paints himself in, denying as he does that if the *a priori* chance of a coin landing heads is $\frac{1}{2}$, then the chance of two heads is $\frac{1}{2}^2$, the two events being independent, hence governed by the product rule.[4] In fact, he says, the coin landing heads at the first toss makes the chance of a second heads more than half—unless, that is, we know for certain that the coin is unbiased.

This illustrates, at the same time as it exposes to criticism, his thesis about new evidence changing but not invalidating the original conclusion. To bring this out, suppose, that I am about to toss the coin twice and that I am in complete ignorance as to its fairness. Then the four alternatives in terms of symbols for heads and tails are given by *hh*, *ht*, *th*, *tt*, each with a probability of $\frac{1}{2}^2$ if the principle of indifference is applied. Now let the probability of a second head given a first head be such that $P(h_2 | h_1) = \frac{1}{2} + 2a$. Then $P(h_2 | h_1) \times P(h_1) = \left(\frac{1}{2} + 2a\right) \times \frac{1}{2} = \left(\frac{1}{2}\right)^2 + a$; but the principle gives $P(hh) = \left(\frac{1}{2}\right)^2$. This prior belief is inconsistent with the claim that after a coin is first flipped, the probability of the same outcome at the second trial is greater than $\frac{1}{2}$. If it were, then I would know in advance that the chance of two heads, or two tails, was greater than $\frac{1}{2}^2$, where this is not only inconsistent with the principle but also incorrect, for I would know nothing in advance about the spinning properties of the coin.

The indication here is that either the principle or the evidential thesis, or both, are at fault. With regard to the thesis, I shall now argue that it is in any case mistaken, and in a way that implicates the theory to which it belongs: that probability is a logical relation between evidence and conclusion. Again we have to ask what this means, or what Keynes means by it, keeping in mind his quoted remark; that 'it is without significance to call a proposition probable unless we specify the knowledge to which we are relating it' But now, this would be an extremely strict criterion if applied, and any proposition that seemed to pass the test would very likely be cheating. For what exactly would count as known empirical evidence and in what sense would it exert logical force? If a bag contains nine black balls and a white ball, this being the sum total of my knowledge of them, then by the principle of indifference I take them to be equally likely to be drawn. But how is this different from an assumption to the same effect?

Well, we have not yet examined that principle, but even if we set it aside we are left with a scaffolding of assumptions on which the claim as to equiprobability depends. For instance, it is assumed that the balls are colour fast, that they are the same size and weight, that with these and other conditions in place each ball will be drawn roughly the same number of times in a series of trials. But how do we know that this will be the case even if all physical criteria are satisfied?

Is it really true that probability is bound so tightly to known evidence that if a particular coin is assumed in advance to be fair, then the outcome of the first toss will negate that assumption? Or is it the case that very often a probability belief, far from being held so tightly, is loosely embraced, and in such a way as to accommodate countervailing evidence? Or, rather, evidence that may count against it, the effect of which is merely to place the belief under tension but continuing to hold. We may, indeed, take this further without undue strain, and in terms of the case just mentioned. For if I take the probability of black to be 0.9 given a white ball and nine black balls, then in a series of trials consisting of a ball being drawn and replaced the outcomes are free to writhe and squirm, as it were, before that initial probability estimate loses its grip. Perhaps after a hundred trials between 80 and 100 blacks will have been drawn, it being of the very essence of the probability system that there will always be a degree of freedom; hence the need for probabilistic analysis of the results, which itself will exhibit the same latitude.[5]

Let us now focus on the principle of indifference, whereby it is axiomatic that equipossible alternatives are equiprobable. Suppose that a bag contains three balls each of which is red, white or blue, the colour proportions initially unknown, and that one ball is to be drawn at random. Then each colour is equipossible, for we have no reason to expect the ball to be red, say, as opposed to white or blue, but we know that it must be one of them. The principle of indifference, or Keynes' formulation of it, now decrees that the three equipossible colours are equiprobable, therefore with a probability of a third. This is the only value by which the symmetry of the equipossible in this context is preserved if one accepts the indifference principle. The problem here, unless we take a third to be the probability of guessing which colour will be drawn, is that it equates with the probability of drawing a particular colour if the bag contains one of each. But from equipossibility nothing follows as to proportion. Clearly, there are inconsistencies here, and they need to be ironed out

It would, however, have to be a very hot iron, one's impression being that the logical probability in question is incompatible with considerations of frequency, as indeed Keynes acknowledges; but for him the creases are all in the frequency itself, his theory already being smooth enough. I have argued that it is no such thing, and all the more so if it can be shown, as in what follows, that the frequency component of a probability judgement is very often present but overlooked.

Suppose that a bag contains a single ball marked with a number between 1 and 100, this being all that we know about it. Then the principle of indifference decrees that since there is nothing to choose between the numbers, $P\ (\textit{not-}1) = \dfrac{99}{100}$, just as

$P(1) = P(2) = ... = P(100) = \dfrac{1}{100}$. It is arguable that for these values to be correct, or even for them to have empirical meaning, they need to be linked to frequency, except that we now have a question as to what the empirical application of $\dfrac{1}{100}$ as a frequency ratio would be. One possibility is that the frequency is that of each number in a series of trials in which numerous bags have their single ball drawn from them. But this is absurd, for it would require of a set of bags containing a single numbered ball that each of the numbers between 1 and 100 was equally represented.

Why is it, then, that it seems counter-intuitive, irrespective of Keynes, to deny that the probability of not-1 is much greater than that of 1? The reason, I suspect, is that we confuse the probability of an event with that of guessing correctly with regard to it; or, better, that to speak of the probability of an event in such cases, if one is to be coherent, is to refer to the probability of guessing. This is shown by imagining circumstances whereby it would be doubted whether these probabilities obtained. Suppose, for instance, that a shifty-looking, character sidles up to us in a pub, explains that the bag she is carrying contains a ball marked with a number between 1 and 100, invites us to bet that the number is not 1, and offers what would be very favourable odds if we agreed that $P$ (*not*-1) is very much greater than $P(1)$. Clearly, we would reject this offer, otherwise there could be no explaining how we had survived long enough to be of drinking age; and it is obvious, too, that our distrust would extend to any situation in which the number or its complement was chosen for us. But if we take the one hundred alternatives to be equiprobable only if we are free to choose the numbers, then this is a standard case of frequency-linked probability, in this instance the probability of guessing correctly, which, approximately or as a limit would be one in a hundred for whichever number was randomly selected and ninety-nine in a hundred for its complement.

It would seem, if this is correct, that in some cases a hidden relative frequency connection may underpin one's numerical probability estimates, this being in line with my earlier remark about analysis illuminating what has hitherto been in cognitive shadow. But Keynes would not agree that this is always the case, though he would accept, indeed assert, to return to a point made earlier, that logical probability theory is incompatible with frequentism. This, as we have seen, causes problems, as with any theory of probability that seeks to sideline the role of frequency rather than to analyse it.

At the moment we are about to examine an apparently very different approach that, according to its proponents, is clearly deductive in the probability relations involved, in this way being similar to Keynes' logical theory. Given the approach in question, a particular feature or event may be likely or unlikely, or even miraculous, relative to some other item, which is known to obtain. Thus it is that we arrive at the theory of non-miracles propounded by R.A.Fisher, who is never less than interesting.

# Chapter 6: The No-Miracles Argument

The no-miracles argument applies to inverse probability, the inverse of $P(a|b)$ being $P(b|a)$. Let me introduce the argument by supposing that a bag contains a hundred balls, 99 of them drawn without replacement, their colours initially unknown, and that they all turn out to be black. Then it seems very likely that the last ball is also black. If we now ask how expecting a black ball is to be justified, then we may argue inductively from the colour of the drawn balls; but appeal may also be made to, as it were, there being no miracles, the general argument running as follows. Consider a situation in which $H_0$ and $H_1$ are rival hypotheses such that an event $e$ is more likely on $H_1$ than on $H_0$; then other things being equal $H_1$ has a greater chance of being true, given that $e$ has occurred. In the present case and on the hypothesis of a hundred black balls originally in the bag, one may be certain that the first ninety-nine will be black; on the hypothesis of ninety-nine black balls and a white ball, the probability is 1%, which is very low. Therefore it is very likely, other things being equal, where this should be emphasised, that the remaining ball is black. The point of the emphasis is to remind us of what is known as the base-rate fallacy, which we shall presently explain and discuss.

The no-miracles argument, or so it would seem, enters into a great deal of our everyday reasoning or provides the grounds for it if required. It is used, too, in support of the predictions involved in scientific theories, for if such a theory is false and the predictions it generates are true, then in some cases it is possible that agreement between observation and theory has to be accounted for as due to chance or in some other unlikely way, this being the null hypothesis, the rejection of which may or may not imply acceptance of the theory, this being one of the issues with which we are concerned. What it does imply is that the findings in question are, as they say, statistically significant.

There is also a use of the argument, particularly by philosophers, to demonstrate that the theories underpinning the hard sciences, given their predictive success, are true, though perhaps only approximately. What the no-miracles argument (NMA) does not do, according to Fisher and others, is to exhibit a standard connection with relative frequency: although the probabilities of event *e* relative to particular hypotheses may themselves be thus connected, this is not true of the inference by which we pass from those probabilities to the conclusion that some of the hypotheses are more likely to be true than others. This inference, it will be said, is deductive, so that the notion of intrinsic logical probability enters into the NMA, which is to say that the relation between premiss and conclusion is again one of entailment or partial entailment, this time not based on the principle of indifference.

But note, given the vagueness of the notion of partial entailment, that arguably very little hangs on the question of logical status, this being in line, too, with our system-based approach. And, indeed, with common sense, for why should we not say that the link between probability and frequency or proportion is itself partially entailed? Hence the intuition we all presumably have: that if, in the case of 99 balls drawn, they all turn out to be black, then this probabilifies the remaining ball being black. Given the universality of that intuition, it is hard to believe that it may be justified only by appeal to the NMA; for the fact is, after all, that in the present case the NMA superimposes itself on frequency-based probabilities independently calculable.

Keeping that in mind, let us now turn to what Fisher has to say. In his book *The Design of Experiments* (1935) he attempts to anchor induction in hypothetic inference by considering cases in which a hypothesis is based on successful predictions. He discusses the example of a woman who claims to be able to discriminate by taste between tea in which milk has been poured first and tea in which it has been poured last. To test this claim two versions of an experiment are designed, our concern being with the simpler of the two, such that the ingredient order for each cup of tea tasted is decided by the toss of a coin. If the null hypothesis is that the woman's guesses are correct by chance, then the probability of this for *n* cups of tea is given by $P = \left(\frac{1}{2}\right)^n$. If, for example, $n = 8$, then $P = \dfrac{1}{256}$. Since this is a very low probability, or so the argument goes, it is reasonable to discount the null hypothesis in favour of the woman's claim being correct.

It is possible, of course, that the proportion of correct guesses will be less than 100% but greater than expected as random happenstance, and that is why, according to Fisher, we have to decide in advance on what is to count as an acceptable significance level. To illustrate what this means, suppose that the woman places three out of the 8 cups in the right category, the probability of which is about 21% on the null hypothesis. If the significance level is set at 5%, which is a standard setting, then it follows that a success rate is to be regarded as favouring the woman's claim only if the null hypothesis probability of its being a chance result is less than 5%. This rules out acceptance of her claim on the basis of 3 out of 8 correct answers. One of the more obvious difficulties with Fisher's approach in the present case is that the issue of underdetermination would seem to be an obstacle to acceptance of it, for it follows not at all from the woman's apparent gustatory ability that it really does account for her discriminatory powers in the matter of milk first or last, even if the possibility of random lucky guesses is ruled out. For we are left, after all, with the possibility that she is cheating, or—an extreme case— that she is both sincere and mistaken.

This brings us to Colin Howson and *Hume's Problem* (2000), in which he discusses Fisher and the NMA, whose use in the tea-tasting experiment he takes issue with for several reasons, one of which concerns the difficulty of ruling out alternatives to the woman's claim if the null hypothesis is considered. He gives a list of possible ways in which the woman might know the answers, most of them by way of cheating, and continues, 'By the rules of chance the chance of a 100 per cent success-rate in repeated experiments with the eight cups if the null hypothesis is true is the total chance of all these alternatives. And we are back again to trying to calculate something that does not seem calculable.' (p.51)

## 6.1: The Base-Rate Fallacy

Howson's concern is not only with limited probability application but also with what is known as the base-rate fallacy. In the present case the mistake, or so he would claim, is that of rushing to probability judgement without ascertaining the prior probability of the null hypothesis in the form of, for instance, the woman subliminally registering non-gustatory indications that favour one possibility over another. To prove a point, he invites us to consider a different case, the gist of which is as follows: suppose that an urn contains 999 white balls and 1 black ball, which together with 50 of the white balls is marked with the number 1.

Let "1" mean "ball is marked with the number 1" and suppose that a ball is drawn from the urn. Then $P(1|w) = \frac{50}{999} \approx 5\%$, and $P(1|b) = 1$. Now suppose that the ball is marked with a 1; then according to the no-miracles argument, says Howson, we should reject at the 5% significance level the hypothesis that the ball is white. In fact, he says, $P(w|1) = \frac{50}{51}$ and $P(b|1) = \frac{1}{51}$, since there are 51 balls marked with a 1, only one of which is black. (p.53)

Now, a problem with this counter-example is that it is obvious that Fisher, along with everyone else, would agree that $P(w|1) = \frac{50}{51}$ and $P(b|1) = \frac{1}{51}$. To see what this indicates, we need to compare the example and the Fisher experiment at several points. First of all, take the null hypothesis in the experiment to be, as before, that the woman's claim is false and that her answers are correct by chance. Then if this hypothesis is ruled out, it is for two connected reasons: the first is that there is no prior reason to accept it; for instance, it is not the case that we are in the later stages of an experiment in which hitherto the proportion of correct answers has been no better than chance. Secondly, the outcome of the experiment gives us a reason for rejection, namely that all or most of the woman's answers have been correct, contrary to what would be expected if her claim was entirely insubstantial.

Let us now make a comparison with the Howson example. Here the null hypothesis is that a ball drawn from the urn is white; this is to be rejected only if the same two conditions are satisfied: first, that there is no prior evidence in its favour; second, that there is a reason to reject it, this being furnished by the evidence of the ball drawn from the urn. In fact, there is very strong prior evidence that a ball drawn from the urn will be white; namely, that the urn contains 999 white balls and 1 black ball. Also, there is no *a posteriori* reason to reject the hypothesis, since a ball turning out to be marked with the number 1 is in fact very strong evidence that the ball is white. Since it is clear that the two examples are dissimilar in crucial respects, we should ask how the one informs the other with regard to their interpretation.

The Howson example is, in fact, a standard case of conditional probability, one in which the calculus of chances operates over prior probability values. To be able to evaluate it as impugning Fisher's thesis, we would benefit from a simpler example than Howson's. Suppose again that a bag contains 100 balls, 99 drawn and found to be black. If the hypothesis under test is that all the balls are black, then the null hypothesis is that there are 99 black balls and a non-black ball, say a white ball. Let the first hypothesis be $H_1$ and the second $H_0$. Using the usual notation, we have $P(b_{99} | H_0) = 0.01$ and $P(b_{99} | H_1) = 1$. Fisher would now say that $H_0$ is to be rejected on any reasonable significance test; for instance, one that is based on a 5% limit. The ground for this rejection, moreover, is that on the null hypothesis it is intrinsically improbable that the last ball to be drawn should be the white ball.

For Howson's criticism to be brought into play, we now have to modify this example in order to incorporate prior probabilities. Suppose that the bag is one of 200 bags in a box, 199 containing 99 black balls and a white ball, the odd one out containing 100 black balls. Armed with these initial values we may now use the conditional probability formula and thereby obtain: $P(H_0 | b_{99}) = \frac{199}{299}$. If we call this $\frac{2}{3}$, then although $P(b_{99} | H_0) = 0.01$ and $P(b_{99} | H_1) = 1$, so that the no-miracles argument would favour $H_1$, the initial values make it about twice as likely that $H_0$ is the case. Fisher would now maintain that the inherent improbability of the null hypothesis has been "overweighted" by the introduction of these values.

What this indicates is that if the point of the Howson example is to expose the invalidity of the no-miracles argument, then it fails in that attempt, for Fisher's rejoinder would be that the argument derives its force from the intrinsic probability of events irrespective of prior probabilities. If these are present, then this permits the application of the conditional probability formula or Bayes' Theorem, as with our modified example, the effect of which is to yield posterior probability values, which again is an exercise in the intuiting of intrinsic probability relations. Fisher's scheme of things, in other words, accommodates Howson's proposed counter-example, which therefore has to be considered in the more general context of his rejection of the NMA, central to which is his thesis that probability evidence must exhibit itself as outweighing all the countervailing possibilities, which it cannot do if only some of them are placed on the scales.

The problem here is that such a requirement would be unfulfillable, yielding as it does to the assumptions which any probability judgement, not to mention any belief about anything at all, demands to be made if one thing is to be predicated of another. In the case of the tea-tasting experiment, it is possible that the woman is cheating, and no doubt it would be sensible to safeguard against that risk in all the standard ways. But this is not the same as estimating a probability, and if this, too, is required, then what of the assumptions that enter into the estimation? Should they, too, have their probabilities ascertained? And what of the further assumptions thus generated? …. And so on.

If such a process is not to vitiate itself, then a criterion is needed by which it may be self-limiting; but what could it possibly be, given that the assumptions that enter into its application must themselves comply with it? In practice one could not even specify all the possible ways in which the woman might be cheating; for by what principle might the list be compiled? Well, only serious possibilities need apply; but this merely shifts the problem, for what would be the exclusion rule and how would the neglecting of only slight probabilities be justified? This all concerns deception, but the same point could be made very simply in terms of memory; for if the myriad memories to which the experiment owes its existence all need to have their probabilities checked, then this applies to those involved in the checking and so on.... Clearly, Howson's argument should be rejected; for belief belongs within a system in which the epistemic prerequisites of believing anything at all must obtain by default.

But if, on the other hand, the woman was exposed as a member of the Magic Circle, or if she insisted on being present when the tea was made but promised to keep her eyes closed, or if she aroused suspicion in some other way, then the possibility of cheating would be actively investigated—though still not, one might add, with a probability estimate in mind. Relevant here is the fact that one would not be surprised if cheating was involved, though astonished, one easily imagines, to learn that the woman is both genuine and mistaken in the claim that she makes. Since this is a bare possibility, hard to give content to, incoherence would be the price of entertaining it. Note, too, that the same is increasingly true of the lucky-guess hypothesis as the trials progress, at least if the woman continues to be able to ascertain the correct order of events. In that case her claim will be checked against the more obvious ways in which she might be cheating, for instance by blindfolding her or blocking her ears or confiscating the battery-powered device that she uses to stir the tea.

## 6.2: The NMA and Science

Our present finding is that we should reject Howson's total probability argument against the NMA as a basis for the approximate truth of science and the justification of inductive inference. He has other arguments, one of which concerns the claim that the remarkable predictive power of quantum electrodynamics compels the conclusion that it must be at least approximately true. Consider, he says, the much-trumpeted fact that the theory is accurate to several significant figures in the value it yields for the magnetic moment of the electron, from which the proponents of the NMA as justificatory of science infer that the probability of such a chance matching of theory and observation is correspondingly extremely low, just as the consequent presumption in favour of the truth of the theory is correspondingly high.

Taking issue with them, Howson points out that if a magnetic moment estimation is correct to a particular number of significant figures then it ranges over an interval, which he writes as $10^{-k}$, where the "k" exponent indicates the number of significant figures after the decimal point. Thus: 3.416 correct to two significant figures = 3.42 exactly because the third digit is $\geq 5$. But if, the other way around, we start with 3.42 and are told that it is a number rounded to two significant figures after the point, and if we denote the original number by "x", then the error interval is given by $3.415 \leq x < 3.425$. Hence the $10^{-k}$, or $10^{-2}$ in the present case. To arrive at a probability, we now have to consider the total possibility space, and this, according to Howson, is where the difficulty lies.

For in theory the possibilities range over the whole of the positive real number line, or, more realistically, the domain of positive integers; but either way the set of such numbers is mathematically infinite. Probability theory, at least from a philosophical perspective, is much exercised by the concepts involved, for there are circumstances in which a fraction with an infinite denominator is equated to zero; but we would not wish to say that a theorist's chance of arriving by pure luck at the value of the magnetic moment of the electron correct to several significant figures is no chance at all. What we actually say will depend on the view we take of the notion of countable additivity and its application, which Howson now harnesses to his rejection of the NMA defence of scientific realism.

This, however, is where the horses on the upper deck begin to be spooked, for it seems to me that Howson is needlessly technical in his approach, and that in any case the point he makes about the magnetic moment example does not support his general argument. His counter-example, after all, concerns the problem of infinite possibility spaces in probability theory, or that of division by infinity or zero in mathematics. It may therefore be circumvented by keeping clear of this particular maelstrom and anchoring the NMA thesis in calmer waters. Consider, then, the standard formula for the vertical height of an object in free-fall; namely $h = 0.5gt^2$, where the constant acceleration under gravity is given in metres and seconds, or seconds per second, as $g = 9.8$ m/s$^2$ and $t$ is the time taken for the object to fall to the ground. If $t = 10$, then $h = 0.5 \times 9.8 \times 100 = 490$ metres.

In this example the downward spirals of the very large and little are easily avoided if the NMA thesis takes advantage of the natural constraints that experience places upon ignorance. If, for instance, an object is dropped from a tourist-class hot-air balloon, then very likely its altitude is at most a few thousand metres. It follows that if the claim is that by means of the formula one can calculate the initial height to the nearest metre, then the odds against being correct by chance are thousands to one, which is all that is needed for the point to be made. One is entitled, however, to ask what this unlikelihood could mean in practice, in view of which we may imagine the claim being tested, very much as in the case of the tea-tasting woman, but this time involving the balloon, a stopwatch and an altimeter. Suppose, then, that a physics postgraduate claims to be able to divine the initial height of an object in free-fall, and by the apparently magical device, given only that he is told the duration of the descent, of making marks on paper—or, as he would say, of calculating from a formula. And now an experiment is performed in which the balloon soars into the sky until, or so we may imagine, it comes to rest, whereupon the altitude is recorded at the same time as the stopwatch in its protective box is activated and dropped from the gondola's rim.

Back on Earth shortly thereafter one finds that the student, now armed with a reading from the retrieved stopwatch, which was designed to stop recording upon impact, arrives at a height estimate and hands it to the experimenter. They look on, the student slightly bemused, as an assistant acts as control and delves into a large bag and picks at random a numbered ball, which is also handed over so that a comparison can be made. Clearly, not many people would find the suspense almost unbearable as they waited for the experimenter to adjudicate on which was the closer estimate; or if so then there could be no explaining how they had lived long enough to be of thinking age. But now, the very fact of the discontinuity between use of the formula and the method of blind chance militates against the NMA thesis being able to exhibit the importance of the null hypothesis, despite the central role that is claimed for it. This is what we are trying to establish, to which end we should perhaps return to the business of analysis, starting with the features that the present case and that of the magnetic moment of the electron share with each other and with formula-based knowledge in general, but not so much with the deliverances of the tea-tasting woman.

Note first that everyday certainty attaches to the epistemic source of the student's estimate of the initial height of the stopwatch, which clearly and objectively derives from the formula, the method being that of ascertaining a value for one parameter, in this case $t$, in order to calculate the corresponding value of the other, in this case $h$. Thus it is that if we assume the repeated correctness of the free-fall formula suitably constrained, then either it is pure happenstance, which in terms of necessary conditions is impossible, or the formula has genuine application and is thereby vindicated if we take it, rather perversely in the context of a system, to depend for its validation on the NMA thesis.

## 6.3: Return to the Tea-Tasting Woman

The example of the tea-tasting woman is by comparison rather unfortunate, for it is all too easy, as we have seen, to think of explanations other than hers if one suspects her of cheating, against all of which the possibility of chance correctness is very quickly ruled out as the number of trials increases. At the 5% level, indeed, one may decide after only five trials that the woman is not correct purely by chance, since the ratio here would be $1:2^5 \approx 3\%$. To claim, as we have already seen, that the NMA thesis overlooks the need to determine probability values for countervailing alternatives, is itself to neglect the distinctions between cases that our present excursion into analysis points up. Gustatory claims while sipping tea are subjective, whereas tipping stopwatches over the side of a glorified hamper basket is a publicly observable event; and most people can learn how to use the formula but perhaps not to discriminate by taste between milk poured first and poured last.

There are circumstances, that said, in which the distinction lapses, for instance if the woman, or another woman, claims to be able to discriminate not by taste but by sight. She has trained herself, she says, to detect a difference in the patterns made by globules of milk at the tealine on the inside of the cup, depending on whether milk or tea is poured first. If she is able to impart her observational ability to the experimenter, then any doubts he may entertain will evaporate, and much more quickly than the tea.

What I would like to do, now that a falling timepiece has landed in the middle of this discussion, is to follow the concentric circles of the ripples thus produced. For the fact, if we return to Howson, is that far from needing to be technical the case against the quantum electrodynamics example is quite simply that the very idea of a magnetic moment is theory-saturated and relies for its buoyancy on other such entities that rise to the surface only within a densely esoteric explanatory system. Theoretical predictions in this field are measured not against observation, unless a monitor screen display qualifies, but against laboratory experiments that register within the system and in terms of its abstract entitles, their existence itself owing much to interpretation.

One may speak, of course, of magnetic moments, perhaps after posing with one's favourite film star; but to know what it means within the stellar orbit of particle physics, one would also

need the concepts of spin and electric charge and electron. These in their turn would have to intersect with other circles, and the same for them if one's understanding is to form by cognitive accretion and thereby present itself as grasp of theory.

The difference this makes is that any appeal to the NMA as vindicating quantum theory via the accuracy of magnetic moment estimates, the puzzling implication being that external support is needed, must thereby extend to the whole of science; hence the claim that scientific realism in general stands or falls if the NMA thesis is called into question. But the notion of magnetic moment belongs within a system in which the validity of quantum theory is presupposed, the existence of electrons and other sub-atomic particles being subsumed under the theory itself. Moreover, and again in line with the notion of a system, if the sciences need external underpinning, then so does empirical knowledge in general. There is no demarcation line by which everyday reasoning may be distinguished from scientific inference, such that the latter but not the former needs bolstering by the NMA.

Speaking of everyday inference, I am reminded of the earlier mention of magic formulas, the everyday epistemic also being magical, even without benefit of decimal points. What is also puzzling, picking up on the use of that word in the previous paragraph, is that predictive accuracy to a million significant figures, or whatever it was, is thought to be a significant figure in itself, whereas in fact one might as well adduce the sorcery involved in my predicting that our garden shed will be found to contain a box of 35 mm marbles. What are the chances of my guessing that such an object lies therein? Vanishingly small, one might think, thereby establishing the evidential strength of my astonishingly accurate prediction. One does not wish to seem to boast, but the marbles turned out to be 35 mm correct to two million decimal places.

And in what, exactly, did that evidence consist? Well, I distinctly remember placing the marbles in a box in the shed this morning. But this, as already explained, is epistemically tantamount to my belief that the action took place; and such a belief cannot be supported by anything stronger than itself, since all such support relies on memory and would itself need support. I simply *have* the belief about marbles in the shed, this also being true of my belief that there is a shed and a garden, and of any other beliefs by which my belief about the marbles is framed.

Consider again the proposition that the distance/time formula for an object in free-fall, given by $h = 0.5gt^2$, certifies itself epistemically by successful prediction, the aim being to see how far we can inflate predictive success in its confirmatory role before we have to rely on the NMA to achieve lift-off. If, having become airborne, we did not need it at all, then either it is full of hot air in a bad way or its utility will continue to elude us until, that is, we land once again in the field of probability mathematics.

Time, then, to revert to the previous field, that in which the gravity law is being tested the same as before, except that the experimenter has now been promoted to the position of Keeper of the Magic Formula, in which role he is able to try the method in question for himself, unlike in the case of the tea-tasting woman. This, however, is a significant change of person from third to first for it is only within a system of connections and necessary conditions, in other words a constrained system, that the experimenter can doubt that he is calculating from the formula the initial height of the stopwatch, given that he knows how long it took to hit the ground. We are dealing, after all, with avowals, so that again there is an obvious link with chapters in the previous book, as befits a system-based approach, in particular the chapter on avowals and the earlier critique of Wittgenstein on intentionality. Speaking of constraints, it is only in very limited and containable ways, the details of which would be hard to conjure, that the experimenter would be able to doubt the existence rather than the correctness of his reasoning; but we are supposing, as regards this latter, that his reasoning is correct.

Where does this leave the NMA or the NMA thesis in the present case? The answer is in the experiment-assistant's hands, one of which he uses to draw a number out of a bag, so that it may be compared with the formula-derived height value, any similarity with which is entirely adventitious. Does this not prove that the derived values cannot be correct by chance? But this is to assume that proof is needed, whereas it just is a fact that even in the initial trials the possibility of chance correctness does not arise, a contrast here being with the beginning of the tea-tasting experiment. This is an instructive contrast, for we know that there are many areas of scientific research in which a particular finding may be tested for statistical significance, the null hypothesis cut-off point usually being set at 5%.

The reasons for this particular value are historical, but it would in any case be determined by individual or group fiat as opposed to being entailed, or partially entailed, by the logic of the probability calculus. Indeed, among students of the social sciences there are organised mutterings about making the level stricter, perhaps nearer to 1% than to 5%; and the reason, I gather, is that too many papers of questionable value are being published on the strength of research findings deemed statistically significant at the 5% level. Again, then, frequency considerations arise, albeit in the diluted sense in which a probability method may be judged by its predictive success.

## 6.4: Logical Status of the NMA

What, though, of the NMA as logical argument? To give content to this, imagine again that 99 black balls are drawn from a bag, the chance of which if the last ball is white is 1%, this being the null hypothesis. Do we really wish to say that this probabilifies not at all the last being black? What if there were a million balls, all but one of them drawn, each of them black? Compare this with complete ignorance as to the colour of the balls before any of them are drawn. The inference from 99 or 999 or 9999... balls drawn and found to be black to the last being black would seem to involve frequency; but on the other hand the NMA, if one is familiar with it, may give formal expression to a deduction that it seems perfectly natural to make. Spontaneously, and with no prompting from philosophy or science, we may reason that if the bag originally contained a solitary white ball, then very likely it would have been among the 9 drawn, or the 99, or the 999..., our conviction increasing with the number of balls.

There are two connected further points to be made, the first of which is that if the NMA applies in the present case when there are 9 black balls drawn, then it must also apply to 99, as to 999 and so on, and with increasing likelihood. The second is that it may be possible to establish a direct connection between the NMA and frequency. The idea is that we consider a complete set of alternatives and apply the following rule: that if there are initially $n$ balls in the bag, the colour of the remaining ball will be taken to be that which predominates in the $(n-1)$ ball sample. What needs to be proved is that the success rate, as measured by the proportion of correct predictions as to the colour of the last ball, compares favourably with the probability of guessing correctly, which is 50%.

Let there, to begin with, be 100 balls, such that "$b$" denotes black and "$w$" white and let the colours be given by numerical subscripts; thus $b_{25}w_{75}$ indicates 25 black balls and 75 white. Here is the first entry, featuring an all-black sample:

$b_{100}$; $P(b_{99}) = 1$. This translates as follows. Given 100 black balls in a bag, the only possible sample is 99 black balls, the ball remaining in the bag predicted to also be black. Thus it is that the probability of a correct prediction is 1. To continue:

$b_{99}w_1$; $P(b_{99}) = \dfrac{1}{100}$, this being the chance of incorrectly predicting a black ball still in the bag; whereas $P(b_{98}w_1) = \dfrac{99}{100}$, this being the probability of a correct prediction of black.

$b_{98}w_2$; $P(b_{98}w_1) = \dfrac{2}{100}$, this being the probability of an incorrect prediction.

$P(b_{97}w_2) = \dfrac{98}{100}$, this being the probability of a correct prediction.

$b_{97}w_3$; $P(b_{97}w_2) = \dfrac{3}{100}$, this being the probability of an incorrect prediction.

$P(b_{96}w_3) = \dfrac{97}{100}$, this being the probability of a correct prediction

And so on, the last entry being that in which there are 100 white balls at first in the bag, with 99 drawn. Thus it is that for large numbers of balls the method is for the most part effective and with a higher success rate than random guessing could aspire to, provided that the initial state is not that of colour equality, in the present case with 50 black and 50 white balls.

That it is effective becomes apparent if, in trying to understand these results, one begins not with the samples but with the possible initial states, in the present case all 101 of them if the list is completed, which I leave as an exercise. Try to imagine that for numerous trials you employ the above method of predicting whether the last ball is black or white, given that another individual fills the bag and is free to decide on the colour proportion. Let this individual be a malicious demon who is trying to catch you out but is not allowed to choose equal numbers of each colour. Then you win and it loses.

I shall have more to say about this kind of justification of method when I tease out the wider implications of the insights we have gained. Time, then, to gain more of them, courtesy of the Reverend Thomas Bayes.

# Chapter 7: Bayesian Inference

One sometimes is told that an effective defence of Bayesian probability method consists in parading its undoubted successes; but is it successful only in the sense of gaining ground over its rivals? If a virus of a particular kind is keenly competitive and attains epidemic status, one should not favour it over the opposition for that reason alone. There are health factors to consider, and some theorists are worried by what they regard as the spread of an intellectual disease, against which they seek to develop a vaccine. In so doing, they imply a comparison with the rude health of rival methods: perhaps they pit Bayesian against frequentist. But better, in my view, to bring the notion of a system to bear on both of them; for we do, after all, have a wider and deeper aim that goes beyond the partisan. It is wider in that it encompasses probability theories in general, with Bayesian inference the last on our list before we survey them as a whole; and it is deeper in more than one way.

Firstly, I shall try to show that there are forces at work that are hidden, not microbially but in relation to method. Secondly, and at ultimate depth, where the metaphysics of consciousness is located, my aim will be the fittingly impossible one of illuminating impenetrable darkness. In the meantime there are patients to be seen, our first step being to derive Bayes' rule from its origins in the conditional probability formula $P(A|B) = \dfrac{P(A \cap B)}{P(B)}$. So $P(B|A) = \dfrac{P(B \cap A)}{P(A)}$. Since, by the commutative rule $P(A \cap B) = P(B \cap A)$, one may readily derive the rule in its simplest form: $P(A|B) = \dfrac{P(B|A) \times P(A)}{P(B)}$.

Now suppose that there are three bags in an ejection machine, each containing five black balls and white balls in unknown proportions, a bag being ejected and a ball drawn from it. And now a Bayesian posits that the bags are equally likely to be selected, which equates with being equally likely to be ejected, about which he has not the slightest inkling, so that we seem to be back with the principle of indifference. Very likely, however, this would be denied, its place taken by a subjectivist account, which we shall presently consider in detail.

In the meantime, let the three bags be A($b_5$), B($b_3w_2$) and C($b_1w_4$), a bag being ejected and a ball drawn from it and replaced, the bag being returned to the machine. For a subject, if we think of this as an experiment, the aim is to infer from sample to bag. If he now draws a ball and notes that it is black, this gives

$$P(A|b) = \frac{1 \times P(A)}{1 \times P(A) + 0.6 \times P(B) + 0.2 \times P(C)} = \frac{5}{9}$$ if the bags

are taken to be equally likely to be drawn. In that case the priors, each equal to $\frac{1}{3}$, cancel out. Similarly, it will be found that $P(B|b) = \frac{1}{3}$ and $P(C|b) = \frac{1}{9}$, these being the posterior probabilities. Also $P(b) = P(b|A) \times P(A) + P(b|B) \times P(B) + P(b|C) \times P(C) = 0.6$. This is known as the total prior probability, in which the priors do not cancel out.

The following table, known as a Bayes box, sets out in tabular form the steps by which the posterior probabilities are derived from Bayes' theorem:

| Model or hypothesis (H) | A ($b_5$) | B ($b_3w_2$) | C ($b_1w_4$) |
|---|---|---|---|
| Prior probability | $\frac{1}{3}$ | $\frac{1}{3}$ | $\frac{1}{3}$ |
| Likelihood: $P(b|H)$ | 1 | 0.6 | 0.2 |
| Posterior: $P(H|b)$ | $\frac{5}{9}$ | $\frac{1}{3}$ | $\frac{1}{9}$ |

Table 1

Classic Bayesianism is characterised not only by carefree positing of priors but also by a subjectivist account of probability, which I shall now address, lest my attempt at critical analysis fall on the stony ground of our neglect of it. If the theory is that probability judgements are subjective, it cannot be in the truistic sense that if I have a probability belief I experience it as mine, since this is the case with anyone's belief about anything. Perhaps, then, in the sense that my concern is with the way in which the world seems to me. But as opposed, one might ask, to the way in which it seems to whom, exactly? What is usually said, in fact, is that the sense is that in which probability judgements are a measure of degree of belief. And now the difficulty is that of giving content to these words, and in such a way as to counter any criticism. What could be meant by probabilistic degree of belief, given that it goes beyond the subjectivity, in the context of a person as an individual, of belief in general?

One answer, harking back to Frank Ramsey, is that betting odds provide a measure; but all that this does is to pass the parcel to not much effect; for the non-Bayesian, too, is able to appeal to waging a bet. If I take it in the present case that bags A, B and C are equally likely to be picked, this is a proposition about a state of affairs, and it is because I believe it to be true, rather than what I mean by it, that I would accept 2:1 odds if I bet on a particular one of them, say bag A. But in so doing, I accept that in a series of trials bag A would be selected about a third of the time. We shall have to revise that statement, but it may stand for now.

What if, however, there turns out to be a hundred bags, so that $P(A) = \dfrac{1}{100}$, and yet I continue to accept the 2:1 odds? Then it will be said of me that I do not understand betting odds, or probability expressed as a fraction, or probability per se; or that if I do understand them, then I am not betting in order to win. If I try to explain that I am a subjectivist in this matter, so that the odds I favour express my degree of belief, which I ascertain by a process of inward belief introspection, or by waiting to see what odds my mouth comes out with, then the bookies involved will no doubt be planning that Caribbean holiday they never thought they would be able to afford more than twice a year.

Clearly, there are rather large obstacles to embracing a subjectivist account of probability theory, which would have to be such as to ground its proponents' practice. Since they seem to me, given that requirement, to ground it in a quagmire, it should be possible for this fact to be extricated. To that end, one might simply point out that probability concepts accommodate both subjective belief, to which one can always give an objective gloss, and objective chance, with the demands that it makes on subjective understanding— except that these two instances of the use of "subjective" are pleonastic. I suspect, indeed, that one uses it to refer, somewhat misleadingly, to individual epistemic variation, whereby it is able to gain purchase because people differ in the evidence, and the strength of it, by which they support or derive their probability beliefs, which also differ but only within the constraints imposed by one's grasp of probability concepts

Another possible defence is to claim that the positing of priors, whether equal or not, is a methodological tool, its utility misconstrued by the anti-Bayesian sceptic. Writing about the use of that tool when priors are assumed, Andrew Gellman (2013) denies that Bayesians 'believe their assumptions rather than merely treating them as counters in a mathematical game'. Since he goes on to say that Bayesians 'make strong assumptions and use subjective knowledge to make inferences and predictions that can be tested by comparing with observed and new data', I fail to grasp how it is that an assumption can be both a genuinely held belief and a mathematical chess piece—and, indeed, I am also being obtuse about the implied difference between subjective and ordinary knowledge. But I know what it is to make a prediction, for instance about drawing a black ball or about colour proportion in a series of trials, and it is not the same as playing with numbers and symbols

Still treating of rejoinders to scepticism about Bayesian priors, consider the claim that the offending priors will always, at least in theory, be swamped by the data if numerous trial are conducted. By way of response, we shall treat of the general case in which the number of trials will vary, the posited priors being different for each bag, the mathematics involved being that which attaches to binomial distributions. If $p$ is the probability of drawing a black ball and $q = 1-p$ that of the ball being white, then for present purposes the random variable of interest is the number of black balls drawn in $n$ trials. In the general case of $r$ black balls drawn the probability function is given by $P(rb,(n-r)w) = {}^nC_r p^r q^{n-r}$ where ${}^nC_r = \dfrac{n!}{r!(n-r)!}$. But since we are supposing that only black balls are drawn, so that $r = n$, the formula reduces to $P(nb) = {}^nC_n p^n q^{n-n} = p^n$.

Imagine, the same as before, that a bag is chosen and that the number of each type is unknown, but let there be no presumption as to the bags being equally likely to be drawn, so that $P(A)$, for instance, can take any value, not just $0, \dfrac{1}{3}, \dfrac{2}{3}$ or $1$ depending on the number of type-A bags. Alternatively, let the Bayesian subject claim that he has a particular degree of belief, which then translates into a prior for $P(A)$. Actually, the qualification is

usually made that the belief, or the degree of it, has to be reasonable; but this is a caveat, one might think, that lets the cat out of the vat.

Be that as it may, we now consider the general case in which the priors are claimed to be $x$, $y$ and $z$, the number of trials being given as $n$, so that initially $P(A) = x$, $P(B) = y$ and $P(C) = z$. Then $P(A|nb) = \dfrac{P(nb|A)x}{P(nb)} = \dfrac{x}{P(nb)}$. Since $P(B|nb) = \dfrac{0.6^n y}{P(nb)}$, an inequality obtains if $x < 0.6^n y$, for instance if $x = 0.5^n y$. So for any number $n$ of trials, and for any prior probability of B, there is an infinite range of prior probabilities of A for which the

conditional probability of A is less than that of B, so that, in the sense in question, B overpowers A; or, as Fisher would say, the greater proportion of black balls in A relative to B will have been overweighted. Clearly, one's choice of prior does matter, the Bayesian having yet to prove otherwise.

Now let him argue that he is free to choose a value of $x$ for which the overweighting will fail for the number of trials that he has in mind. Far from rebutting the sceptic, however, this is to capitulate to him; for the whole point is that if one is free to choose priors then this freedom extends to making one hypothesis more probable than another as opposed to ascertaining it objectively.

My present concern relates to the claim, which I have attempted to rebut, that priors can always be overweighted if enough trials are conducted and their outcomes are one thing rather than another. We rejected that claim, but in any case one might ask 'What of it?' and in the tone of voice by which one gives the same reply when told that a fair coin will converge to equal numbers of heads and tails if the subject begins the experiment at an early age and relies on her longevity to be able to complete it. The fact is, after all, that her interest is in the present behaviour of the coin, not its propensities in the long term.

So far, there is much to be sceptical about with regard to the Bayesians' treatment of priors, but eventually we shall have to place the issue in the wider context of Bayesianism in general and probability theory as a whole, the sceptic about priors then being required to eat a balanced meal. The main course, now that the starters are mostly disposed of, will concern what I shall refer to as the sampling problem, which again will spill over into the general theory of probability. We shall focus, that is to say, on data in relation to inference, and eventually we shall revisit the problem of the priors.

## 7.1: Discrete Distributions

Let us begin, still treating of discrete random variables, by considering not the three bags but only bag $C(b_1 w_4)$, our aim being to present what I shall refer to as the first sceptical argument: one by which the sampling problem is partially constituted. Let us take it that the Bayesian subject, unaware of the identity of

the bag, knows only that there are five balls, black or white, and that they are equally likely to be drawn. If he is asked to estimate the colour proportion parameter on the basis of a single trial, then quite likely he will initially take the colour alternatives $b_0 w_5$, $b_1 w_4$, $b_2 w_3$, $b_3 w_2$, $b_4 w_1$, $b_5 w_0$ to be equiprobable. If we now suppose that a black ball is drawn, so that the Bayes box is as above, then the equal priors cancel out and partially determine the posteriors: if they were not equal they would not cancel out.

Since they do, the posterior ratio—the product of the ratio of any two posteriors and that of their priors—reduces to the ratio of the posteriors. If we take the second posterior in relation to the last, then the second should be rejected, the rule being that one posterior trumps another if it is much greater, a ratio of at least 3:1 sometimes being agreed upon, as in the present case. The rationale is that a black ball is more likely to be drawn from the bag containing more black balls. If the choice is between $b_5 w_0$ and $b_1 w_4$ then the former is favoured.

| number of black balls | 1 | 2 | 3 | 4 | 5 |
|---|---|---|---|---|---|
| Priors | $\dfrac{1}{6}$ | $\dfrac{1}{6}$ | $\dfrac{1}{6}$ | $\dfrac{1}{6}$ | $\dfrac{1}{6}$ |
| Likelihood: | $\left(\dfrac{1}{5}\right)$ | $\left(\dfrac{2}{5}\right)$ | $\left(\dfrac{3}{5}\right)$ | $\left(\dfrac{4}{5}\right)$ | $\left(\dfrac{5}{5}\right)$ |
| Prior × likelihood | $\left(\dfrac{1}{30}\right)$ | $\left(\dfrac{2}{30}\right)$ | $\left(\dfrac{3}{30}\right)$ | $\left(\dfrac{4}{30}\right)$ | $\left(\dfrac{5}{30}\right)$ |
| Posterior | $\dfrac{1}{15}$ | $\dfrac{2}{15}$ | $\dfrac{3}{15}$ | $\dfrac{4}{15}$ | $\dfrac{5}{15}$ |

Table 2

Since they do, the posterior ratio—the product of the ratio of any two posteriors and that of their priors—reduces to the ratio of the posteriors. If we take the second posterior in relation to the last, then the second should be rejected, the rule being that one posterior trumps another if it is much greater, a ratio of at least 3:1 sometimes being agreed upon, as in the present case. The rationale is that a black ball is more likely to be drawn from the bag containing more black balls. If the choice is between $b_5 w_0$ and $b_1 w_4$ then the former is favoured.

This, however, is where the difficulty lies, for the actual source, which is bag C, is the one that is given as the least probable, and the proportion least like the actual as the most probable. Clearly the sceptic can make hay with this, but we have to ensure that the gate to the field is locked so that the Bayesian cannot easily escape. Might he clamber over it, one wonders, by relaxing what seems to be an implicit chronological rule, hence the term "prior", by which the priors are to be decided upon before, in the present case, any balls are drawn? One could easily attack this aspect of the Bayes box method; but our concern for the moment is to take it seriously, as Gellman does: 'it seems like a cop-out and contradictory to the Bayesian philosophy to estimate the prior from the data' (2013).

The point being made is that the subject cannot justify the method he uses by appeal to the steps by which he applies it in any particular case. The justification would have to be in general terms, as we shall presently discover; but this is to imply that the subject, although he is following the steps by which the method unfolds, is working in the dark, this being one of the ways, again as we shall presently discover, that the method belongs within a system. In the meantime, what should we say if the anti-sceptic appeals to the more technical aspects of Bayesian or general probability theory? Since no mention has been made of continuous distributions, perhaps now is the time to take them into account. I suggest that we start with the basic idea of a continuous random variable tracing out a curve, where this will replace point estimates and running up and down the steps of a histogram.

## 7.2: Continuous Distributions

For our second sceptical argument, we start with black or white balls in a bag, their proportion unknown, the task of the Bayesian being to estimate the probability of a black ball being drawn. He will need hypotheses, each of which will assign a numerical value to H, the probability parameter, with prior probabilities attaching to them and forming a probability distribution. Conceivably, he now sets out a row of eleven equally spaced possible probabilities of black: 0, 0.1, 0.2, …0.9, 1, each facing its prior in the next row. But if gradations of 0.1 then why not 0.01, or 0.001 and so on? Taken to a limit, the transition would be from a probability mass function to a probability density function, such that measures are taken on intervals. The pdf would be given by:

$$P(a \leq X \leq b) = \int_a^b f(x)dx$$ if X is a continuous random variable.

By way of illustration, let $f(x) = 2x$ be graphically outlined as in Table 3, which is not to scale. The area under the line represents unity if the gridlines register gradations of 0.1 on the x-axis and 0.2 on the y-axis. Then we may speak of, for instance, the probability that $X$ lies between 0.4 and 0.5, this being the area under $y = 2x$ delineated by vertical lines between these x-coordinates and the diagonal. This gives $0.5^2 - 0.4^2$ and clearly the sum of such areas is unity. Note that any intervals may be considered, not just those that are defined by grid lines. The integration available is not necessary in the present case, or not if one is able to use geometry to work out the area under the line between two points on the x-axis. Integration is quicker, that said, the method being as follows. Since it is given that $f(x) = 2x$, $\int 2xdx = x^2 + c$ from the formula $\int ax^n = \dfrac{ax^{n+1}}{n+1} + c$. The constant "c" drops out if two points, d and e, are taken, the area then being $e^2 - d^2$, for instance $0.5^2 - 0.4^2$, the same as before. The linear pdf $f(x) = 2x$ is mainly illustrative here, the standard kind being that which attaches to uniform distributions, these being represented by a line parallel to the horizontal axis.

Many other pdf's are curves, as with the Normal distribution, the point being that with continuous random variables the posited

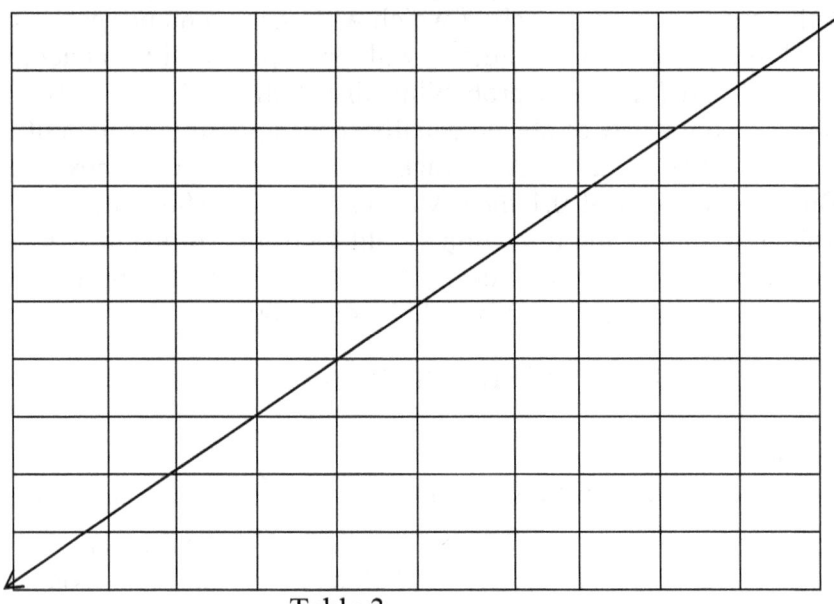

Table 3

model is very likely one of several standard forms on offer, so that again the issue is that of justifying the choice that one makes.

So much, then, for the possibility that continuous probability distributions are more resistant to criticism than those that are discrete. If anything, one might think, they are equally vulnerable, if only for the reason that although a particular curve determines which points are on or off it, the converse is not the case; for a point or set of points is consistent with an infinity of different curves. Illustrating the argument in terms of the present example, consider two points, say (0, 0) and (0.5, 1), one's aim being to fit a model to them. Wishing to keep it simple, one chooses the present linear function, on which the two points are indeed to be found—but also on, for instance, $y = 4x^2$, which describes a parabola, the general expression being given by

$2y = 2ax^2 + 4x - ax$ for a suitably restricted infinite range of values of $a$.

Since the issue we have raised in connection with modelling hypotheses to data is not without importance, we need to pursue it further now that continuous distributions have been introduced, the place to start being with maximum likelihood estimates, which will involve the processing of data beyond posterior ratio cut-off points. Such estimates are interesting in their own right, but also the present issue attaches to probability theory in general, not just Bayesian inference. We are treating, after all, of the possibility that even probability theorists may lose their grip on a distinction that is easy to hold in theory but slippery in practice: that between matching the data to a model and a model to the data. The following, then, is our third sceptical argument.

## 7.3: Maximum Likelihood Estimate

In *Bayes' Rule* (2013) James V. Stone uses the example of a biased coin to introduce the notion of a maximum likelihood estimate, the coin being such that $P(heads) = 0.6$, this being un-known to the subject, who is told only that after ten tosses the coin has shown seven heads and three tails. With coins the usual practice, based on most of them being fair, is to factor their likely fairness into the prior distribution model; but Stone's concern is with the MLE method of estimating probability, to which end he considers the likelihood function $P(x|\theta)$ where $x$ is the given data and $\theta$ the probability of heads, such that $P(7h, 3t | \theta) = \theta^7 (1-\theta)^3$ for $0 \leq \theta \leq 1$. Here the binomial coefficient drops out, the probability being that of seven heads followed by three tails. The MLE is found by using the differential calculus as follows. Let $y = \theta^7 (1-\theta)^3$; then $\dfrac{dy}{d\theta} = 3\theta^7 (1-\theta)^2 (-1) + 7\theta^6 (1-\theta)^3$. Since this equals 0 for $\theta = 0.7$, which corresponds to a maximum value, the MLE is given by $(0.7)^7 (1-0.7)^3 = 0.0022$. Stone points out that it is not a coincidence that the value of $\theta$ by which $P(7h, 3t | \theta)$ is at a maximum is the same as the proportion of heads by which the data is constituted. What counts at the moment is that for Stone the MLE given by $\theta = 0.7$ is an estimate of the true probability of heads with this particular coin. But the true value, namely 0.6, plays no part in the calculations and is known only because it is the value that he specifies. It is by tossing this coin, he says, that the data were generated; but the fact is that it might have had a different bias and still produced the outcome of seven heads and three tails, or the same or no bias but a different outcome. If, in this latter case, the outcome had been three heads and seven tails, the MLE would have been $\theta = 0.3$, the likelihood given by $P(3h, 7t \mid \theta = 0.3)$ =0.267. Also, $P(3h, 7t \mid \theta = 0.6) = 0.04$, which is low, but so far we are ignoring the possible significance of improbability of outcome for a given value of $\theta$.

But surely, it might be said, there must be ways of allowing for error and uncertainty; and indeed there are, for instance if confidence intervals are considered. But they all need data and results to operate on, such that if these are misleading, then methods involving a spread of probability values will start from the wrong point on the curve. It is clear that in such cases the method of confidence intervals is about as much use as a pram at a hen party.

Where does this leave us? The remaining defence would be to withdraw to the citadel of arming oneself with further data by conducting more trials. But one could never know when to sound the retreat, for there need be no indication that the sample is leading one into an ambush. On the contrary, the MLE or posterior ratios light up the trail ahead and cast all other routes into darkness.[6] There is, in any case, another reason why the present sceptical thesis would apply even if more data were derived. Suppose, in order to bring it to bear, that the coin is tossed a further ten times; and now we simply state that the outcome was four heads and six tails, which gives a total of seven heads and thirteen tails. There is no need to work out any of the new probability values, for the point is already clear enough. The essence of it is that the subject is, in a sense that needs clarifying, working in the dark, which is to imply that the unseen world must be such as to enable him to move about, so that he is not aware, the analogy now losing its bearings, of lacking a compass.

Time, then, to delve into the question of interrelations between sample and population, or between instance and rule, the first step being to remind ourselves that the sampling problem transcends the different theories and methods that we have brought under scrutiny. What we seek is an account by which the validity of such inference may be established, and in such a way as to accommodate the successes and the failures of reasoning of that kind. Without it, after all, there could be no probability calculus with physical-world application; and what this indicates is that necessary conditions will enter into the account that we give.

## 7.4: The Probability of Success

Consider the following table in connection with estimating the colour proportion of balls in a bag containing three black or white balls from which single balls have been drawn and replaced five times. Here the top row displays the colour alternatives for the balls in the bag, and the left-hand column those for the sample.

The connection between the two sets is illustrated in the central cell and explained as follows. The probability that the sample consists of two blacks and three whites given one black and two whites in the bag is, in terms of the binomial formula, $\left(\frac{1}{9}\right)\left(\frac{8}{27}\right)(10)$, which is to say that $P(b_2 w_3 \mid b_1 w_2) = \frac{80}{243}$. I have omitted the probability fraction denominator, which is always 243, as too the binomial formula workings, leaving only the numerators.

| colour proportions | $b_0 w_3$ | $b_1 w_2$ | $b_2 w_1$ | $b_3 w_0$ |
|---|---|---|---|---|
| $b_0 w_5$ | 243 | 32 | 1 | 0 |
| $b_1 w_4$ | 0 | 80 | 10 | 0 |
| $b_2 w_3$ | 0 | 80 | 40 | 0 |
| $b_3 w_2$ | 0 | 40 | 80 | 0 |
| $b_4 w_1$ | 0 | 10 | 80 | 0 |
| $b_5 w_0$ | 0 | 1 | 32 | 243 |

Table 4

Recall that our concern is with certain difficulties impeding the inference from sample to source. Table 4 displays the likelihood values by which the opposite inference— that from source to sample—smoothly unfolds. That is: we shall not find fault with it for the moment. Indeed, we could by means of it arrive at estimates based on the following principle: that the favoured source alternatives will be those that most probabilify the sample. The sampling problem is now that of justifying this principle, to which end a partial resolution may be forthcoming if we consider Table 4 as a whole, not just a particular sample and possible source. Suppose that we take such a source, say $b_1 w_2$, and conduct a thousand trials in which a ball is drawn and replaced five times. Then the sample will be given by $b_1 w_4$ or $b_2 w_3$ about 640 times, for each of which the principle will dictate that we choose, correctly, $b_1 w_2$ as the most likely source. Put another way, the probability of success will be about 0.64, which is greater than we might expect from guesswork. This is also true of the other three sources and the samples taken from them.

That said, it is only up to a point that the sampling problem is resolved by appeal to the probability of success. This is mainly because the method uses probability to resolve the problem, which is itself probabilistic. The aim, however, is to descend below that level, the need for which will become clear when we now trundle another sceptical argument into the arena. Our tactic so far has been to show that a subject cannot know whether his inference from sample to source will hit the right target. The new argument strikes more to the centre and radiates outwards.

Suppose that eight otherwise identical balls in a bag are tagged A, B, C, …H, the presumption being that they are equiprobable, this being tested when balls are drawn and replaced a hundred times. Now take it that ball A is drawn twenty times, the others occurring much less frequently and more in line with the ideal expectation of twelve to thirteen times, keeping in mind that the total is 100. Then one's impression that ball A finds it easier than the others to exit the bag may be blocked by the following consideration: that if the experiment is taken to be part of a much larger one involving a thousand trials, then 20 out of 100 is perfectly consistent with 125 out of 1000. And in the case of the others, say bag B, one readily conceives of 12 out of 100 turning into 200 out of 1000, these being the proportions if bag A moves closer to the norm and bag B further away.

This indicates that the probability calculus is beset by evidential conflict or inconsistency if the wrong kind of question is asked. It concerns a fundamental principle of selecting between hypotheses, which are judged according to the degree to which a sample is probable when conditionalised upon them. And it is just this principle that our connected sceptical arguments have thrown into disarray. But also, I earlier maintained that the Bayesian use of priors is problematic, this needing to be emphasised before alerting the notion of a system to the present urgency.

To that end, I suggest that we return to the central cell of Table 4, such that $P(b_2 w_3 | b_1 w_2) = \dfrac{80}{243}$. What, though, of $P(b_1 w_2 | b_2 w_3)$?

Using Bayes' Rule in the form $P(a|b) = \dfrac{P(b|a) \times P(a)}{P(b)}$, and

letting $x = P(b_1 w_2)$ and $y = P(b_2 w_1)$, one finds that

$$P(b_1 w_2 | b_2 w_3) = \dfrac{P(b_2 w_3 | b_1 w_2)}{P(b_2 w_3)} \times x \text{ such that } P(b_2 w_3) =$$

$$P(b_2 w_3 | b_1 w_2) \times P(b_1 w_2) + P(b_2 w_3 | b_2 w_1) \times P(b_2 w_1).$$ It may

then be shown that $P(b_1 w_2 | b_2 w_3) = \dfrac{2x}{2x + y}$.

If $x = y$, the probability is two-thirds, so that one is faced with the difficulty of justifying the equation. It just is a fact, after all, that there are many cases in which the priors all have different values. Perhaps there are numerous bags, some with all blacks, others with two blacks and a white, and so on, the numbers of each kind known in advance of choosing a bag at random. What the above example demonstrates is that priors matter, even to the point where a conditional probability may be written exclusively in terms of them. Time, then, to mount a defence against the sceptic.

## 7.5: System, Sub-System and Resolution

If we start with the notion of equiprobability, the sceptic asking how we know that the five balls are equally likely to be drawn, then we may invite him to test them. If he labels the balls a, b, c, d, e, the results of numerous trials may be as follows: a, c, a, e, b, d, d, e, e, a...a, a, b, c, d. But what is he to make of such a sequence? Not much, or not unless probability theory itself is brought to bear; for we know that relative frequency is probabilistic. If analysis corroborates that the balls are equally likely to be drawn, this is of interest only if expected to continue if the sequence is extended, or if the balls are similarly exercised on other occasions. Put another way, each ball is expected to be equiprobable with itself, so that its frequency in relation to the other balls will exhibit stability. Hence its being said, at least by me, that the sceptic rejects equiprobability in one form only by cleaving to it in another.

Whether he is inconsistent in so doing will depend on his reasons, which perhaps he is able to ground in the difference between the two cases. I said earlier—an initial statement subject to review—that one may know nothing of the prior probabilities of the three bags in an ejection machine: but what does this acknowledgement of ignorance imply? Perhaps that one should conduct the relevant investigation before drawing any balls from the bags; but how far should this be taken if the machine is not to grind to a halt?

Recall that if a bag contains 100 balls, 99 drawn and found to be black, so that very likely, or so it seems, the last one is, then appearances may be deceptive. One may have no idea whether or not the bag was picked at random from hundreds of such bags, or how many of them contained 99 black balls and a white ball. But still, it is very likely that the last ball is black.

Now suppose that one is shown an ejection machine, its numerous bags each containing either 100 black balls or 99 black and one white. Under instruction to estimate the proportion of each kind, one presses the eject button in order to accrue data, which one then enters into a Bayes box in which equal priors are posited. This may be understood in terms of equipossibility and Keynes' thesis that probability is relative to evidence, the relation being logical by nature. But better, in my view, to construe it in terms of a probability sub-system of conditions and connections.

Such an approach commends itself because probability theory and application rely on processes of reason and confirmation that set their standards within, as we have seen, the sub-system itself, in which respect it is partially closed. This helps to explain why it is that the judgements and estimates involved are underdetermined by the evidence, as indeed is all belief, the reference being to the wider system of our knowledge of the world.

We now return to the sampling problem and its close links to the notion of underdetermination. The link within a system is to necessary conditions, the scaling principle, as I call it, being such that the favoured source is that by which the sample is most probable. This principle, with all its technical refinements, is necessary to the application of the probability calculus, the nature of things being such that the principle is validated within the system itself. To see that this is indeed the case, try to dispense with it when inferring from sample to source.

What are the ramifications if the question of Bayesian priors is re-examined? I showed earlier that $P(b_1w_2 \mid b_2w_3) = \dfrac{2x}{2x+y}$, where $x$ and $y$ stand for the prior probabilities of $b_1w_2$ and $b_2w_1$ respectively. If there is a prior reason why $x$ and $y$ should take different values, then they have to be factored in; if there is not, then the Bayesians may choose to equate them. One thereby implies equal relative frequency in a series of trials, but such frequency itself belongs to the probability system or sub-system, as do the methods of ascertaining it. Clearly, the prior evidence of inequality has to have weight, despite the casual approach of some practitioners. Equating the priors would yield a value of two-thirds for the posterior probability $P(b_1w_2 \mid b_2w_3)$, and this, too, would be subject to frequency checking, again within a partially self-validating probability system. Partially, that is, because the high posterior probability, if it obtained, would manifest itself in an obviously large number of $b_1w_2$ bags offering up the $b_2w_3$ sample in a series of trials. Obvious, that is, even to those who are ignorant of probability theory.

Since equal priors continue to pose a difficulty, the present analysis needs to be taken further. A significant point is that probability estimates very often are not subjected to a reality check, the question of frequency confirmation not being on the agenda. If it is required by the method used that priors are to be equated, in the present case that $P(b_1w_2 \mid b_2w_3) = \dfrac{2}{3}$, then this is the value that will obtain in any further application and in the calculations involved therein. Now combine this with the thesis that the probability sub-system is partially closed. Also, and relatedly, that meaning can be given to the notion of the general probability of success of a method that seems to fail in any particular case, as with the scaling-up principle. Again, that sceptics about Bayesian priors have to contend with the universal fact of underdetermination, and in particular with assumed equiprobability being intrinsic to probability theory. Yet again, this being a new argument, that a theorist may be more in agreement with Keynes than I am, and more accepting of the thesis that the probability relation may be one of entailment, or partial entailment. The theorist may then appeal to such a relation in his defence of the positing of equiprobability among equipossible alternatives. This goes far beyond the positing of priors, for instance into the default position that the six faces of a die are equally likely to turn up when the die is thrown.

Whether they are equal or not is, according to A.J.Ayer, a matter of non-logical fact, believing as he does that relative frequency is empirical. On the contrary, I have argued, it is a probability concept; but there still is a question, now being addressed, as to whether one is entitled to assume equal probability if nothing indicates inequality. My approach has been indirect, the question not so much answered as placed in context, the issue thereby resolved insofar as this is possible.

Ludwig Wittgenstein would perhaps interject at this point that the application of probability theory constitutes a practice, as in "this is what we do", the emphasis being on use and technique. My preference is for the notion of a system of connections and necessary conditions, but with assertibility conditions always in the background. I have not highlighted these latter, partly because they do nothing to deepen the analysis or dissipate any fog. If in treating of the problem of perception, one says that if it looks like a duck, quacks like a duck and waddles like a duck, then it is a duck, then the identity goes no deeper than the criteria by which its credentials are confirmed. If it looks, quacks and waddles like a duck, this being what one observes, the problem of perception is just that of what it is to be, or to perceive, a physical object, such as this one.

That said, there are points of contact with Wittgenstein, for instance with his thesis, on one interpretation, that we follow rules blindly. What I mean by this, however, insofar as I agree with it, is that a rule partakes of the intentional, the seat of which is in the non-conscious. When, for instance, one draws 99 black balls from a bag, on which basis the remaining ball is taken to be very likely also to be black, the deeper rationale for that near-certainty is hidden from view. In the same vein, one learns how to use a Bayes box, with or without equal priors, thereby arriving at a posterior probability estimate. But awkward questions are easily asked, faced with which one is at a loss what to say. And the same, more generally, in the matter of underdetermination, a sceptical approach to which might easily undermine our beliefs about anything at all. Fortunately, it is this universality that rebounds against the sceptic, which is to say that he refutes himself. Necessary conditions enter at this juncture.

## 7.6: Conclusions

It would seem to be fundamental that the application of so many key concepts may be rendered uncertain by the asking of awkward questions, not only about probability theory but also elsewhere. How can processes of perception be both objective, a window revealing the physical world, and subjective, the glass reflecting sensory experience back at us? One answer emerges from the sceptic's failure to convince, which extends to any form of sceptical solution to the problem of perception. What it demonstrates is that it is by re-asserting our everyday perceptual scheme, but from the upper deck of philosophical analysis, that the strictly unbelievable is avoided. The sceptic, however, pretends otherwise, and shouts from the crow's nest that an iceberg is dead ahead.

It is a mirage in a seascape of over-chilled sceptical argument, or so I tried to show. My method was that of steering perceptual illusion, so beloved of the sceptic, into the wider seaways of the many shipping routes in which the appearance of an object may vary according to conditions. The discontinuity between subjective and objective does not thereby sink beneath the waves, but from the bridge it is not a threat; rather, it is a mystery.

With probability, too, a similar challenge may be issued to the sceptic, who is required to take a broader view of the sampling problem, merging as it does into the panorama of underdetermination in general. Also incorporated is the problem of the priors, which thereby becomes less acute, the context being that in which the assumption of equiprobability is intrinsic to the probability calculous.

Scepticism yields to analysis, one might say, and it deepens when extended to cover consciousness and the myth of conscious adequacy, such that one is obliged to postulate a hitherto undiscovered realm of the non-conscious. It is to this uncharted place of profundity that much of one's perplexity about perception, intentionality and probability may be referred. Further analysis along these lines will be found in *Beyond Knowledge*. What has not been dealt with at all in that work is the problem of personal identity, an omission that will now be rectified,

# Chapter 8: Personal Identity

Conspicuous by its absence in *Beyond Knowledge* is any discussion of the problems of personal identity, or indeed any mention of their being susceptible of a system-based approach. Wishing to make amends, I should perhaps outline what seems to be the main problem, which is that of what it is that personal identity consists in. Taking a wider view, it would seem that a parallel difficulty manifests itself in the lack of consensus among philosophers as to the approach one should take in seeking a solution. A first-person approach may suggest itself, the crucial question being that of what I mean, or should mean, when I claim ownership of particular experiences in the present, past or future tense.

Nowadays the preference is for an externalist account of what it is to be a person; but for me a cold air enters when the door of my identity is left open, my natural inclination being to shelter from it in the inner citadel of my subjective self. The fact is, in any case, that the question of what I mean or how I know requires an answer, and even the externalist will have to address it if his theory is to carry conviction. In the meantime, there are the wider issues to be brought under scrutiny, the lack of common ground among philosophers being itself a significant fact, perhaps signposting the possibility of an entirely different exit from otherwise irresolvable personal identity issues. If we begin with David Hume, there is, as always, disagreement as to interpretation, in the present case in relation to his views on the identity of persons, objects and events. One of the main exegetical questions, according to Xiaomei Yang (1998), is that of whether Hume is a sceptic about identity, given the distinction he seems to make between perfect and imperfect forms of it.

This latter is taken to correspond to the changing and interrupted nature of one's experience of the physical, a question immediately arising as to whether any other kind of observational unfolding of events is possible. If not, then the notion of perfect identity would seem to have no everyday application, referring as it does to an ideal that is difficult to even conceive of except as a form of Platonism. We distinguish, it is true, between specific and numerical identity, this computer monitor being numerically the same as the one I used a minute or a month ago. But this does not preclude interruptedness or change, for instance when I switched it on just now, the screen lighting up, and lost sight of it for a moment when I blinked.

No wonder, then, that there is an exegetical difficulty with regard to Humean scepticism, for it is not even as if the notion of identity invariably transcends the fact of change. Rather, the more fitting concept is that of a system in which judgements of sameness and difference may vary in semantic content from one circumstance to the next. It may be, for instance, that we are able to trace a plant in bloom back to a particular seedling which we say that it once was, thereby implying identity; but what it means in this case is that they are connected by a process of development and change, our grasp of which informs our use of "the same". If a photo of the original seedling and the present plant were juxtaposed, we would not say that they were identical, since clearly they are not, but we might say that they are the same in the sense just explained—or, rather, this would be understood, the explanation not needed.

There are implications here for the analysis of the notion of personal identity, but at present our concern is with physical objects and events. Speaking of which, we referred just now to sensitivity to circumstance, as illustrated by the fact that we would not say that a match head before and after ignition was the same, though this would be said about a car before and after a crash. The suggestion is that identity concepts are complex in application and belong within a system.

If we now return to Hume's coupling of change with observational interruptedness, this latter seems fundamental to what it is to perceive the world, in view of which we may ask whether it has the sceptical import that Hume seems to attach to it. Looking at a rose in all its glory, I may be distracted in any number of ways, perhaps admiring an even showier specimen nearby; but whatever the distraction, it would not normally occur to me to read into it a difficulty about the concept of identity.

Similarly, and in applying identity concepts in everyday life, we are fully aware of change and interruption, and yet we still say that the same object may come under different descriptions at different times, or even at the same time if perspectival change is very sudden and quick. What we are understandably ignorant of is the perfect/imperfect distinction itself, quite possibly because it has no application. In fairness to Hume, however, we now need to place this discussion in the wider context of his empiricist epistemology. My point is that the support it gives to his views on identity must be weighed against their counter-intuitiveness when the arguments we have set out are placed on the scales.

## 8.1: Hume's Empiricist Philosophy

According to Hume, the world that we register through the senses presents itself as a sequence of impressions, presumably similar to sense data or qualia, these being the perceptual data that the mind, if Hume is correct, fleshes out in the form of ideas of physical objects and events. An impression of physical identity would have to be unchanging and uninterrupted, corresponding to the idea of the physically identical if we had one. Since, however, there is no such impression; we can have no such idea, the challenge for Hume being to explain how we nevertheless count it among our belongings. This is one of the junctures at which Humean psychology comes into play, suggesting as he does, on one interpretation, that the imagination creates a fiction: that of physical identity itself. One's perceptions, he says, are bundled together by causal relations and by those of resemblance and continuity, and this, for Hume, is a basic empiricist principle at work: so basic, in fact, that he extends it to what may seem to be the unrelated sphere of personal identity.

Thus it is that one has no simple impression of the self, the gap being filled by imagination, which arguably Hume takes to mislead us, the same as in the case of our conception of the physical world. Introspection, it would seem, fails to reveal a self of any kind, whether simple or complex, changeable or invariant, and exhibits the mind, rather, as a sequence of impressions of heat or cold, pain or pleasure, and so on.

Speak for yourself, one is tempted to retort, and indeed very little of this is beyond dispute, as attested by the fact that much of it is disputed, in which connection Yang cites Penelhum (p. 197), who detects in Hume a sceptic about identity, a somewhat opposing view being expressed by Ashley and Stack (1974), They take Hume to distinguish between identity of the perfect and imperfect kinds, about which we ourselves have taken a sceptical stance. Since we have already engaged with these issues, albeit very briefly, what I suggest is that we prolong the engagement, but with less obsessing about what Hume actually meant, my treatment of the various arguments being more impersonal. We shall continue to show some interest in whether Hume would embrace them, this time not in the front stalls but in the back row, which by convention and lighting is where embracing is expected to occur.

If we start with the principle in question, we know from previous chapters, themselves an extension of the work on perception in *Beyond Knowledge*, that the empiricist treatment of perception is to be rejected in favour of a system-based approach. What it yields is that perception is intentional, where this includes its being inferential, and that we see an object-part as being perception-independent and objectively real. Integral to perception thus characterised is that we may identify the part as being the same at different times, depending on the observational circumstances.

But surely, it might be objected, the difference between impression and idea does correspond to perceptual reality, at least in the sense that we may distinguish between the perceptually given and that which is inferred. But this is not what Hume had in mind by "impression" and "idea", and in any case the correspondence is illusory, for instance if I look at this monitor screen, which is virtually the only part of the monitor I can directly see from this chair. For my registering of the screen is itself a matter of intention and inference, with essential links to memory and expectation. This will be more perspicuous if we suppose that a continuously changing number sequence is displayed, so that the display is different from one moment to the next. Clearly, it is only through memory and expectation that we become aware of the sequence, the same being true of our moment-by-moment seeing of the screen itself, a momentariness which does not depend on the screen changing in appearance as opposed to looking the same for long periods, this latter also being a case of perceptual processes unfolding through time. So much, then, for perfect and imperfect physical identity being distinct. That said, there are parallels between Humean sceptical theory and the notion of a system at least on some planes; but my conclusion was that they diverge too much on others for the parallels to be informative about three-dimensional reality.

Returning to perfect and imperfect, our dismissal of difference has ramifications, the defeated distinction yielding to the thesis that imperfect identity does not have a superior counterpart elevated above it but is, on the contrary, the only kind of identity that actually obtains. There is, as already agreed, a comparable distinction: that between specific and numerical identity; but this, too, falls victim to the arguments used against perfect versus imperfect sameness between objects. Imperfect identity, then, may hold between two instances of an object subject to change in one form or another, depending on the circumstances. What the issue is really about, given the vagueness of saying that one thing is the same as or different from another, is the use of more precise descriptive language to bind or separate objects or events. Since description is necessary to any discussion of the issues it raises, I now propose a more incisive system-based resolving of them.

## 8.2: Scepticism and Consistency

Suppose that a sceptic about identity challenges us to explain why we refer to a broom in a cupboard as *the* broom, thereby individuating it, when we know that last week the handle was replaced and before that the head. Numerically it is not the same, he points out, adding that his own reference to the broom is to the object that has been identical with itself for the past week, so that he cannot be accused of inconsistency. Then clearly the broom's numerical identity does not extend further than a week into the past, but we may still ask whether, as the sceptic maintains, we are mistaken in what we imply when we refer to, for instance, the broom that for years now has been kept in the cupboard. One response is to point out that our references to the broom change not at all after we are told about the new head and handle, for we still say that someone used it a month ago and again yesterday. An enabling condition here is that the cupboard always contains only one broom; and another is that it always functions as one, which it would not do if the stiff bristle broom head was replaced with a soft brush head. Note, too, that the broom, even over the last week, has varied in appearance according to perspective, visual distance and lighting; but we still say that numerically it is the same as it has always been over that period of time. The indication, at least so far, is that we are not in error in our references to the broom.

Consider, that said, the following objection: that the variations just adduced concern appearance, not, as it were, physical essence. This is unaffected, on which basis the broom really is numerically the same, or has been for the last week. So far, there is no error to be exposed, but Hume would argue, the objector continues, that there is no such essential substance to which numerical identity may be attached. The ontology is that of perceptual impression, not physical solidity, this being where the mistake lies, the error arising when imagination switches on, the fiction undetected in such a bright light

As against this, the countervailing argument is that Hume's perceptual analysis in terms of impressions and ideas, this latter notion in the present case replaced by that of the imagination, with its connotations of "imaginary" and "figment", is untenable, yielding as it does to the notion of a system. A system-based analysis, as in *Beyond Knowledge*, reveals that we perceive objects or object-parts as three-dimensional, the new broom sweeping all talk of impressions, sense data or qualia into the bin. It does not follow that the notion of physical essence may be reinstated, and our thesis, indeed, is that the distinction between perfect and imperfect identity is invalid. This, however, does not do justice to the complexity of the case. Just now I contrasted perceptual impression with physical solidity, but that was too simplistic an opposition, for "physical solidity" belongs to everyday empirical discourse, whereas "physical essence" is, or is meant to be, metaphysical.

My position, then, is that "physical essence", if required to be metaphysical, would have no semantic content of the applicable kind. Therefore, it could impinge not at all on the extension of the term "physical solidity"; and the contrast here, since we have rejected Hume's philosophy of perception, is not with "impression" but with some appropriate everyday description, my preference being for "physical event". Then the distinction still standing is that which obtains between solid object, ideally viewed as unchanging in certain circumstances, and physical event, the focus being on movement and change, even if solid bodies are involved.

On one interpretation of Hume, he is guilty of misrepresenting an everyday distinction as a pairing off along metaphysical axes, with perfect or numerical identity equated with physical essence. The axis perpendicular to it would then be that of qualitative identity. Far from its being metaphysical, however, it seems to me that the categories of specific and numerical identity constitute a useful distinction, the emphasis being on utility rather than on any deeper insight to be gained.

By way of illustration, let us allow the sceptic to target not a broom but a fireworks display, for its appearance changes from one moment to the next and the fireworks when spent are replaced by others. In what way, he demands to know, is the display the same over time, such that one is justified in one's individuating reference to it? Clearly, he thinks that there is no such distinction; and yet, he himself refers to the display, for instance when he maintains that it is different from one minute to the next. This time he cannot avoid the charge of inconsistency, which is to say that he has to address it, which in my view is no easy task, at least if he insists that we are mistaken in the identity assumptions that we make. To save himself the toil and trouble, ultimately ending in tears, he could turn from sceptic to scholar and direct his energies along the lines of conceptual analysis, in this case of the distinction between specific and numerical identity.

What we then find in the present case is that we thus distinguish between classes according to particular conditions, the display being identified as a light show in which each firework briefly adorns the night sky. The firework next in line has individual identity until the moment it is lit and launched and perhaps explodes into an expanding sphere of bright stars before extinguishing itself. These aerial pyrotechnics belong to the same display, but if a firework from a nearby separate display strayed into the first one's airspace, then that is the account that we should give of it, the reference being to separate displays. If it rains, we shall say that most of the fireworks fizzled out, thereby ruining the display. If asked about the physical or perceptual composition of the display, we should very likely have to admit ignorance. What are the expanding but ephemeral galaxies of bright stars made of? What would I see if I was inside one of them? And so on.

Turning now to a second example, this time taken from Hume, consider a village church unchanged over centuries compared with another in the next parish that was demolished a hundred years ago, the original stone used elsewhere, and the church rebuilt from new materials? Why it is that the stone being original in the first village confers antique authenticity on the church that is built from it? The everyday answer is just that it is the original church; but its walls, if that is all there is to it, are too slippery for the sceptic to gain purchase. She requires the answer to, as it were, grip tighter on the stone; but the problem here, as we have seen, is that the stone, or a particular block, is imperfectly identical with itself in all the ways to which perceptual variability and interruptedness conduce, not to mention such facts as that perception is intentional, which we have seen to include its being inferential.

But is there not at least one level, perhaps that of the mystical, on which we gaze in wonderment at the church's ancient visage and internal architecture from a bygone age? Indeed there is, just as I behold, the mysticism being that of awed ignorance, this exquisitely thin and tarnished Queen Victoria coin from Barry Island beach, the answers buried for ever in the sand, far beyond the reach of my metal detector. But the questions are mint fresh: How did it get there? Who did it belong to? What of its adventures? Which was the day when it fell or was lost, its last owner grown up or grown old, and finally in mourning at the memory of that summer in the sun?

But this, if it is metaphysics, suffers from transposition of idiom, the mystical being related but not the same. Very well, but mention was made of different levels, perhaps with metaphysics going deeper, its intrusion into consciousness being mystical. We quite commonly feel, or I do when the coin is in front of me on this desk, that we are straining after profundity, or should expect it as we peer down, the metaphor of the sea immediately turning thoughts into waves. Otherwise, after all, there would just be an old coin and me in this room, thin and tarnished as we are, and a rainy window. In fact my feeling is that the metaphysics of the identical, if it obtains, transcends the distinction between specific and numerical identity, which I have tried to exhibit as being in the shallows, the deeper waters being those beneath which, as in *Beyond Knowledge*, the intentional and the non-conscious reside. It remains to be seen whether the concept of personal identity may be analysed as to depth, and whether it inhabits a deeper sea or wider ocean.

## 8.3: Personal Identity and its Problems

According to the Stanford Encyclopaedia of Philosophy there are several issues that the problem of personal identity comprises, prominent among which is the question of what it is that identity of this kind consists in and that of its criteria of application. R.D. Swinburne (1973) is of the view that these two questions are commonly conflated, much to the detriment of adequately answering either of them. The question about criteria is normally taken to apply to the judgements we make about other people, in line with the favouring, already remarked upon, of an externalist standpoint. We shall follow this train until it leads either to water or to the camels collapsing beneath us, this latter event being consonant with our insistence on treating the various problems in this and *Beyond Knowledge* from a first-person point of view.

Returning to Swinburne and criteria, he says that they concern bodily and psychological continuity. There would also, according to Swinburne, have to be relations of resemblance between continuous bodily states, and the same with mental phenomena. Suppose by way of example, the focus being on memory, that I borrowed money from an identical twin, each of them now claiming to be the lender and demanding repayment. How should I determine which is the lender and which the liar? The obvious course of action would be that of interviewing them separately and asking questions the answers to which, others things being equal, would be known only to the lender. How much did I borrow? When was the cash handed over and in what denominations? And so on. At most one of the two would have the correct memories.

There seems nothing objectionable about Swinburne's account of personal identity criteria, especially if we keep in mind that it is always possible to conceive of exceptions to the rule, provided that the rule holds in the general case. If, for example, I wake up to a completely unfamiliar face reflected back at me in the bathroom mirror, my screams awaking my spouse, who joins in, then my reassuring her that I am the same person as before may require several protracted interrogation sessions, not just my answering a few questions. Eventually, however, the criteria satisfied, my identity will be reaffirmed and my name allowed to appear on the divorce papers. In fairness to my spouse, imagine that she discovered that my brain had been transplanted into a younger and fitter body, so that my screaming, or the shock it seemed to manifest, was feigned. There is no problem, at least at the present stage, with any of this in relation to criteria, an omission easily rectified if we now turn to what it is that personal identity consists in.

For the fact is, after all, that the criterial account in the twins case presupposes the application of the notion of personal identity. The question we raised was that of which twin was the lender, not whether the individuals involved were the same on different occasions, this being taken for granted, as indeed it would be in the general case. Speaking of which, there is an instructive comparison to be made between criteria of personal identity and those of mental states as manifested in behaviour. Note that in this latter case, they are not Wittgensteinian in character, there being no relation of partial entailment involved, if that is what Wittgenstein had in mind.[7] Rather, it suits our present purposes to think of them as relating evidentially to mental states, the same being true of relations to personal identity. In both cases, that said, it is possible to go deeper, for there are necessary conditions to consider; but not quite yet.

At the moment, our question is as follows. Will we find that personal identity is presupposed even when we delve into its essential nature? That such enquiries may involve circularity is a possibility that resonates with Swinburne, who now maintains that the notion of personal identity is irreducible, and in the sense that we cannot analyse it into any constituent parts. It is at this juncture that he argues that conflation leads to confusion, the criterial account in terms of bodily continuity and resemblance and memory being unsuitable and misleading if used to exhibit the constitutive nature of personal identity.

Despite Swinburne's convincing arguments against this use, I propose to neglect them for the moment by exploring the possibility just mentioned: that reductive or constitutive analysis of the essential character of personal identity will always tie itself up in circular argumentation in which that identity is presupposed. This brings us to a philosophy journal article by Geoffrey Madell (1974) on A.J.Ayer's theory of personal identity published in *The Concept of a Person* (1973) and presented in the chapter with the same title. In "The Concept of a Person" Ayer argues that experiences are mine if they are centred on my body and causally dependent on it. Responding to criticism, Ayer considers the objection to such theories advanced by Peter Strawson (1979), who detects a circularity in their supporting arguments, about which Ayer writes:

If my experiences are identified as mine only in virtue of their dependence on the state of this body, then the proposition that all my experiences are causally dependent on the state of my body must be analytic; and so the theory is committed to a contradiction' (p.116)

He continues:

There would indeed be a vicious circle if the experiences had first to be identified as mine before it was discovered that they were dependent on my body, but this is not the case. The position is that a person can be identified by his body; this body can be identified by its physical properties and spatiotemporal location; as a contingent fact there are certain experiences which are causally connected with it; and these particular experiences can then be identified as the experiences of the person whose body it is. There is nothing inconsistent in this (p.117)

Madell has reservations about Ayer's rejoinder, pointing out that if there is a causal connection between body and mind then we should be able to independently identify the experiences thus caused. He goes on: 'The circularity which really matters shows itself in self-ascription: I must establish that an experience is causally related to my body before I can ascribe it to myself, but can only do this if I first identify the experience as mine.'(p.51) He is dubious, too, about memory, for it 'presupposes personal identity and cannot serve to define it'.

Keeping this in mind, I suggest that we try to achieve some clarity in these matters, reflecting first on the issue of independence. In snooker a cue ball impacts an object ball, each of them independently describable and their causal connection a contingent one. The connection between experience and subject is, however, more proprietorial, for instance in the case of sensation. Accidentally placing my hand in a vise which I am tightening with my other hand, I feel pain, the point being that I feel it as my pain, a question arising as to whether this impression of ownership is intrinsic to the sensation itself.

How would Ayer or others respond to this? He would say, or the general response would be, that there must be some unifying factor by which experiences on different occasions are predicated of the same subject, and the only suitable candidate is the physically continuous body by which the experiences are generated. This brings us to the question of the persistence of the individual self, usually expressed as follows. Suppose that there is a person P and a person Q on a later occasion: what are the conditions by which P and Q are the same person? A possible answer, as we have seen, concerns continuity, either of the body or of the mind; but a different approach may be suggested if we now take a first-person stance, our intention being to suggest that the question of personal identity persistence, as normally under-stood, is misconceived.

We have seen that the appeal to memory is problematic, and we attached a question mark to bodily continuity and resemblance in the case of my looking in the mirror and seeing a stranger reflected back. These indications will be of interest later, but in the meantime one's impression is that our sense of self is always at hand, reference to which is a first-person authoritative self-ascription of personal identity. Since this is a pivotal point, we need to enquire into what exactly turns on it.

Suppose that I recover consciousness from a coma and initially have no memories at all. Then from the moment I awake I am self-conscious and, if my linguistic skills are also up and about, I may immediately refer to myself in all the usual ways, perhaps asking where I am and what happened to me. We can even take this further if we imagine that I become fully conscious but am completely paralysed; and yet I may reflect on what a fine mess I am in. If my condition improves, where this includes greater mobility and my being able to open my eyes and focus, so that my viewpoint is of myself in relation to my body, then I take possession of it by virtue of the special relation I have to it. I have control over it, albeit limited, and I see through these eyes and hear through these ears, or so my senses tell me, where this includes my sense of sight and hearing. Also, this body is causally linked to my sensations and to other conscious items.

The point, as against Ayer, is that a precondition of my corporeal awareness is that my sense of self should already be in place, as also the awareness, as indeed it was when I first regained consciousness. That is: I did not have to consciously infer to this being my body. A corollary is that personal identity is not autobiographical but is fully formed and intrinsic to human consciousness, even if all memory of oneself in the past has been erased. This view is shared by Galen Strawson (2009), who has much that is of interest to say on the topic. Our shared approach conflicts with Ayer's thesis, following Hume, that introspection does not reveal a sense of self. Mine does, or I am entitled to report that interesting fact if certain assumptions are made, namely those by which Ayer and Hume require the self, if it is to exist, to be an object of introspection.

Hume is of the opinion that 'When I enter most intimately into what I call myself I always stumble on some particular perception or other…and never can observe anything but the perception' (Treatise, 1.4.6. paragraph 3.) What he means is that he is introspectively aware of having a sensation, say, the reference being to 'my awareness of my sensation'. This, however, implies the existence or occurrence of a self. But if, as he claims, he has no acquaintance with a self in the way that he has with a sensation or other impression, then the inference to be drawn is not the sceptical one, unless one is committed to Humean empiricism, but rather that the self is not an introspectible object—or, better, not in the way that a sensation is.

## 8.4: Intentionality and the Non-Conscious

Our finding so far is that criteria of personal identity do not equate with its essential nature, as also that when they are kept separate, according to Swinburne, it becomes obvious that the concept of personal identity is irreducible. This is a thesis to which we are initially drawn, given his arguments and those of our own that we have developed. Since irreducibility does not preclude suitably restricted analysis, I suggest that we return to it in the light of previous findings. To begin with, my thesis in *Beyond Knowledge* was that consciousness is momentary, each moment falling into the void of the past and replaced by the next, the sequence of such moments expanding pyrotechnically into transient spheres, no sooner glimpsed than imploded. They leave behind, it is true, the sulphur smell of memory, but this, too, is fleeting in its way.

What follows, with regard to the intentional, is that it must reside elsewhere, not in consciousness but in the realm of the non-conscious, and it is to here that the question of what personal identity consists in should be referred. That, at least, is the theory, our project being to substantiate it so that it prevails over the reductionist approach. My immediate aim, however, is to show that the puzzling nature of personal identity is appreciated by Hume himself, for instance when he admits to being flummoxed by his own sceptical theory and unable to bridge its explanatory gaps. He writes at one point of 'The essence of the mind…equally unknown to us with that of external bodies' ('A Treatise of Human Nature', 1739, Introduction, para. 8), and he admits that 'My hopes vanish when I come to explain the principles that unite our successive perceptions'….. (Treatise, Appendix, para 20/21). His puzzlement is not the same as our perplexity when we contemplate intentionality and the hidden instruments of the non-conscious; but there is enough resonance to make the comparison worthwhile.

## 8.5: Avowals and First-Person Identity

According to Madell, the first-person predicating of mental states most clearly presupposes the personal identity of the subject, this being a statement that I would find it difficult to disagree with. Let us turn instead to the link between personal identity and the problem of avowals. To see what it is, we first need to state the problem, which was discussed in detail in the avowals chapter of *Beyond Knowledge*. Suppose I say to a person, known as Mr P, that I am hungry, to which he responds not with food but with a challenge to my epistemic credentials. He asks 'How can you state that you are hungry and yet make no attempt to provide any evidence, let alone to justify the authoritativeness of your avowal?' And now there are two points to be made, the first of which is that person P is unwittingly inconsistent, his implied criticism impacting the rhetorical question itself. For how does Mr P know that I said that I was hungry? By way of memory, he will protest, but he made no effort to evidentially support his apparent recollection.

And yet, the statement 'I remember your avowal as to hunger a moment ago' is itself an avowal. Secondly, any attempt on my part to assuage Mr P's epistemic concerns, thereby taking them seriously, will tumble me into the same pit of inescapable underdetermination. If I say that I know that I am hungry because I feel it, I imply not only that my memories are correct but also that I know the meaning of "hungry", just as P would have to say that he, too, is linguistically competent, again falling short of the evidential standards that he himself has edified. It is in this way, by appeal to necessary conditions and self-refutation, that the problem of the authoritativeness of avowals may be resolved.

## 8.6: Surviving the Self

Much of the following concerns a well-known Bernard Williams (1970) article on personal identity, admired for the apparent paradox to which he draws attention. My aim, attention drawn, is to resolve it, and in favour of our own thesis, which we shall pivot on his in order to point in a different direction. Suppose, he says, that two people, A and B, are volunteer experimental subjects.

They are told that after being placed in a machine they will emerge with the A-body now behaving like B, the B-body like A, and that the person in the A-body has B's memories and the converse for the B-body. Person A is asked beforehand whether he wants the A-body after the experiment to be tortured, the person in the B-body to be rewarded, or the other way around. He says that he wants the person in the B-body to be rewarded. This may reasonably be interpreted, says Williams, as convincing evidence that A believes that he will occupy the B-body after the experiment. The point so far, says Williams, is that the experiment indicates that bodily continuity is not the personal identity necessary condition that many philosophers assume that it must be.

He now, rather ingeniously, turns the story on its head, thereby raising some awkward questions about certain assumptions by which the issues are framed. Suppose, he says, that a mad scientist has power over me—note the first-person vantage point— and announces that I am going to be tortured tomorrow, immediately prior to which he will interfere with my brain in such a way as to remove all the memories at present available to me. I am now very afraid, for I can easily imagine waking up after an accident in great pain and suffering from total amnesia. He adds, however, that prior to the pain he will substitute for my genuine memories a set belonging to a particular other person, which I will then register as belonging to me. Williams' point is that my expectation as to these changes tempers not at all my fear that I shall have great pain inflicted upon me, to which they seem to be irrelevant, as the author's detailed analysis indicates.

And yet, he says, there is no essential difference between this case and the original, apart from the way in which they are presented, in particular the change from third- to first- person as the favoured point of view, which he takes to be significant without claiming to know what its implications are. Perhaps we can be of assistance to him, but even without it he has established that a change of presentation, as he puts it, of essentially the same proposition can result in conflicting identity assignments. In the original case person A believed that he would occupy the B-body and thereby avoid pain. In the second, I believe that I cannot avoid pain, despite my knowing that the scientist will have replaced my memories with those from the brain of some other person, call him person B.

If we now render assistance, the significant difference is indeed the change of grammatical person, for I can easily imagine, as Williams can, that I wake up with complete memory loss and in great pain. What, though, if I lose my memories and gain another person's? In the original story person A knew in advance that his memories would be those of the person occupying body-B, which in limited ways would exhibit his personality and character. In these ways, and in wishing body-B to be free of pain, person A is taken to show that he believes that the body switch will actually occur, the body he occupies being body-B. But it follows not at all that he is correct in what he believes, or that he need believe it.

For the other possibility, the apparent paradox thereby resolved, is that A believes, correctly if the machine has done its work, that it has effected a change to his body such that it now resembles body B. This includes changes to his physiognomy, his facial expressions resembling those of B, as also his mannerisms and his general demeanour. As for memory, the original assumption was that A's memories replaced B's in body B; but on the present account there is no such implausibility. The picture we now have is of A retaining his memories, the changes being only to his physical appearance, not his recollections. These changes are perfectly compatible with person-A himself having changed, and the same for any further changes of that kind.

Note for future use that eventually we shall have to be more disciplined in our judgements as to the sense that other theorists make. At the moment we are at the level of uncritical reporting, as with the present example. In the previous paragraph. I mentioned A's memories replacing B's, which I found implausible; but the more incisive point is that of whether anything counts as interpersonal memory transfer.

We shall come to that, but our present insight is that personal identity persists through change; and that it matters whether we take a first- or third- person perspective when we are invited to adjudicate between a person occupying another body as against his identity surviving changes to his own. If this is correct, then the appearance of incompatibility between the two cases investigated by Williams is indeed a function of the different presentations, provided that this use of "presentation" does not rule out the differences amounting to entirely divergent accounts. In the original description we are told that the person in the A-body has B's memories and the converse for the B-body; but this is tendentiously to imply, or to invite us to assume, that the two bodies remain unchanged until their owners are switched.

This, however, is a transformation involving two subjects, not just one, whereas from the standpoint of each the other is not required. Person A, left to his own limited explanatory devices, would note that his body had undergone a change of appearance, his behaviour also having altered, the limits being reached when he was unable to account for these events. At no point would it occur to him that he occupied the body of another person, the sheer unbelievability of which would be enough to deter him from entertaining such a thought. The paradox is thereby resolved.

Let us now prepare to enter in the next chapter a genuine body-swap shop rather than a deeply suspect simulacrum that relies on linguistic manipulation in place of reasoned argument. Suppose that persons A and B consent, both of them bored out of their skulls, to having a brain swap, and that the operation is a success. Then they wake up in each other's bodies and that, seemingly, is that, their notion of personal identity not under any great strain, and each of them the same person, apart from corporeally, as before. There are, however, complications to be encountered, and in addressing them we shall make the acquaintance of Derek Parfit and other like-minded philosophers. In applying pressure to the concept of personal identity, they either reveal its workings or crash its gears altogether, depending on the make and model of the vehicle by which their arguments are conveyed.

# Chapter 9: The Indeterminate Person

In Part 3 of his *Reasons and Persons* Derek Parfit gives a detailed account of his views on identity, these being more concisely expressed in his "The Unimportance of Identity" chapter in *Personal Identity*. My aim will be to critically examine Parfit's thesis about the unimportance of personal identity, during which the notion of a system will be fielded, as will, by way of conclusion, our thesis about intentionality and the non-conscious. For the moment we shall critically examine Parfit's arguments rather than the notions around which they revolve.

He begins by reflecting on the following science fiction events, recounted in the first-person. On Earth my body is destroyed in a teletransporter machine after information about it is beamed to Mars, where my body, including my brain, is reconstituted from organic local materials. Since the person on Mars is a perfect copy of myself, a question arises as to whether it is me or whether I died in the machine on Earth, the visitor to Mars being just a replica of me, where this is to imply numerical difference.

The answer, says Parfit, will depend on personal identity criteria, about which theorists differ. On the bodily continuity view the lack of it precludes the replica being me, to which my comment as author of these words is that continuity should yield to common sense, the sacred cow otherwise in danger of curdling the milk. The better udders are those by which the following principle is expressed: that third-person criteria of personal identity should be subordinate to the first-person perspective as far as the individual involved is concerned.

If we return to his conundrum about the replica, and if I resume my first-person role, having always wanted to visit Mars, it may seem that if breaks in continuity are not an obstacle, then this constructed person might be me. It is, indeed, presented, using Williams' word, as me, the first paragraph ending as follows. 'Examining my new body, I find no change at all. Even the cut on my upper lip, from this morning's shave, is still there.' (p.199) Williams is directly relevant here, for the quoted sentences reveal that its being me is presupposed in the account given, the break in continuity notwithstanding. The point is that my self-reference manifests my personal identity, whatever that may entail and however it is to be analysed. We know that the analysis cannot be such as to strictly preclude continuity breaks, for my personal identity is fully involved in my self-reference. If, for instance, and as I would maintain as author, such reference penetrates to my non-consciousness, then that is what it does when I describe myself as having shaved this morning.

If I say 'I shaved this morning on Earth—oops, I forgot about the continuity break', then there is no oops about it: the "I" in "I shaved" is the same as the "I" in "I forgot", with regard to my referring to myself. In a section (8.1) on "The Subject of Experience" Parfit writes that a reductionist about personal identity can admit that a person is the subject of experiences. He goes on, 'This is true because of the way in which we talk.' If this is a dismissive reference to the use of the first-person singular in the context of the subject-predicate structure of the English language, then it seems to me, rather, that language opens a window onto the self, as in the case of "I shaved" and "I forgot". Since this is a normal use of the notion of personal identity in the first-person, the analysis of that notion must accommodate continuity breaks, and in terms of conditions and connections within a system.

What it must also accommodate is the fact that first-person reference comes under the heading of avowals, the analysis of which is such that they belong within a system to which they are indispensable, as we know from *Beyond Knowledge*. We also established that a condition of their being doubted in particular cases is that the avowals that enter into the expression of the doubt cannot themselves be subject to it.

It is becoming apparent, perhaps, where this is leading, given the earlier indications, the suspense being mild to moderate. If I wake up on Mars, or from a coma, or just from sleep, then immediately I am self-conscious, and if I am amnesiac I begin to collect information and to stake my claim to being a particular individual. If I wake up on Mars, then it is Parfit himself who specifies that I am the person who used the teletransporter machine, not to mention the possibility that personal identity is in any case presupposed. We shall return to this, the main fact for the moment being that my instant self-consciousness is of significance, its implications waiting to be extracted. We have seen that Parfit seems unaware, in his use of the first-person singular, that he thereby commits himself to a particular answer to a question that he regards as being open. That is, if I refer to myself as being on Earth and then on Mars, then the replica is myself, this being presupposed in the account that I give. That out of the way, I suggest that we resume our restricted critical examination of Parfit's theory of personal identity.

He now investigates different reductionist accounts of personal identity, one of which, known as constitutive reductionism, is the view that it consists in physical and psychological continuity but is distinct from them. By way of illustration, he supposes that a group of trees grow together on a hill, in which case we may learn that they form a copse; but we are told that this is information about the meaning of a word, not about the trees themselves. In the same way, he seems to imply, facts about personal identity consist in facts about an individual's body and about various interrelated mental and physical events, such that an individual at one time and an individual at another may be said to be the same person.

His point is that if we know the relevant physical and mental facts about that individual, then there is no further fact in which his identity consists. Note that even so, we may still speak of criteria, for in practice we rely on cues, very often on visually recognising an individual as the person seen previously, the inference going far beyond the evidence, this being the sense in which criteria are involved. Without criteria thus defined, nothing could be known about any external thing. Note again that here he attempts not at all to explain how it is that one may speak of an individual's body and mental states without his personal identity being presupposed.

Approaching a cliff edge, Parfit advances what I shall refer to as the variable cell replacement thesis, such that he asks us to imagine a range of cases of cell replacement, with varying proportions of my body being destroyed and replaced. At one extreme no cells are replaced, my notion of self being unaffected; at the other they all are, so that we are back with my replica. Modifying the original teletransportation story, suppose that having bought a ticket I present myself at the machine, which introduces itself as Alex, who informs me that it is no longer necessary for me to be dematerialised in order to be teletransported to Mars. After I emerge from the machine on Earth I can see myself, according to Alex and Parfit, on a screen showing me in a Martian studio, and I can talk to myself if I wish.

At this point we need to pause for a moment lest we be swept out into space by Parfit's magicking of interplanetary commuting, our critical faculties tumbling off into the void, To begin with, it is myself on Earth, my replica on Mars, and that makes two people, not one. If any exploited native Martians attack my replica, it will be that individual who tries to pull an arrow out of his head, this being the only explanation, in terms of brain damage, for his belief that he is me. This is argumentation of the kind used by Swinburne, who appeals to our personal identity concepts to remind us of what we already know. Parfit, to be fair, does not really deny that there are two people, but he now takes a further narrative step by supposing that the machine has damaged my heart, which will be permanently out of order in a few days' time. His aim is to establish a quite outlandish thesis, which has been seriously considered by many theorists of personal identity. Namely, that my dying and being survived by my replica, who can expect another forty years of life, is almost as good as my own survival, with forty years of incredulity at Parfit's thesis to keep me occupied.

Parfit's argument runs as follows, the first step being to develop the variable cell replacement thesis. At one extreme no cells are replaced; at the other they all are, a replica thus created. But intermediate cases, he says, are not so clearcut, and if some but not all of my cells were replaced I could not be certain in advance as to my personal identity status. Still, one might think that there would always be a fact of the matter, even if it was unascertainable, as to whether the resulting person was me. Parfit rejects this assumption, arguing as he does that there would have to be a demarcation point, with its being me on the one side and not me on the other.

Since this is counterintuitive, one should conclude that such questions are indeterminate of answer. That said, he wishes to qualify that concession, arguing as he does that I am free to respond to them, perhaps by saying that the person now regaining consciousness after the cell replacement operation is myself. This is to be understood, he says, as my choosing one description over another, with only a verbal difference being made. Since this point is not without interest, Parfit invites us, in *Reasons and Persons*, to reflect on the following supposedly illustrative case.

Consider the reductionist view that a person is a particular brain and body and a series of interrelated physical and mental events. He now aligns this view with the notion of indeterminacy, linking them as he does by drawing a parallel with what it is to be a club that undergoes radical change. Let the club members meet weekly without fail until, for whatever reason, the meetings are discontinued. Years later the former regulars create a club with the same rules and the same name as before. Asked whether it is the same club as the original, or an exactly similar club, they may be unable to answer, despite there being nothing relevant that they do not know.

Then Parfit says that the statement "This is the same club." would be neither true nor false and would be an empty sentence. If, however, the members now meet at a different venue, where they are presently convened, the original venue not far away, a newcomer might ask whether it is the same club as the one that used to meet not here but there. This is not an empty question, but Parfit would no doubt point out that the newcomer is not in possession of all the relevant facts. So, is Parfit correct? Suppose I say 'This is the same club or an exactly similar one.' But my statement does have a truth value.

If we set that aside, Parfit now leaves the club armed with insights which, he says, we should apply to personal identity if we are reductionists. The nature of those insights, however, is not at all clear. We can describe cases, he maintains, where 'between me now and some future person, the physical and psychological connections hold only to reduced degrees'. (p.214) In such a case, he says, I can always ask whether I am about to die, or whether the resulting person will be me. For a reductionist there may be no answer, the question being empty; and the claim that I am about to die would be neither true nor false. That is what he says, there being an obvious parallel with the club case; but he also draws a parallel between a person and a nation, where this latter consists in a group of people united in certain ways, the point being that a nation is distinct from what it consists in but is not independent of it.

Similarly, a person is distinct from his body and from his mental content but is not independent of them. It is unclear what "distinct" means here, but in any case it would seem to conflict with the claim, carried over from the parallel with clubs, that once we know about the relevant bodily and psychological continuity (resemblance should also feature), perhaps in relation to a particular individual human being, then we do not gain additional information when personal identity is ascribed to that individual. The reason, or Parfit's reason, is that personal identity consists in such continuity and resemblance. But how, in that case, is the notion of distinctness able to audition successfully when it has been written out of the script?

If this criticism is correct, then in the context of Parfit's analysis it is misleading and perhaps disingenuous to speak of personal identity as distinct from that in which it consists. And if it is disingenuous then this is because he may be using the notion of a distinct entity as a surreptitious proxy for personal identity as a thing-in-itself. Without that notion he is left with continuity in one form or another as that which gives content to personal identity; but the elephant in the room seems to have trodden on that content, for in my own case, at least, my sense of self transcends continuity. I have already advanced that thesis in the case of bodily continuity and resemblance, and I can readily imagine that I awake from a coma with no personal recollections to my name.

The point is that this would detract not at all from that self-awareness which gives every sign of surfing the waves of my conscious mind. Whatever the criterial role of the continuities in question, they are not criteria at all from a first-person standpoint in the present tense. Such comments, however, belong to system-based analysis of the concept of personal identity, and we still have some way to go if our aim is to establish its credentials and promote it over the heads of Parfit and those who share his views.

Time now to move on, the way forward being to circle back to the variable cell replacement thesis in order to examine Parfit's arguments in support of it. He says, it may be recalled, that if no cells are destroyed and replaced with new ones during the operation, if that is how we think of it, then I am the same person as before. But if all my cells are replaced, so that I am a replica, then I am not, according to Parfit, the same person as before. Therefore, there must be intermediate points that have one thing in common; namely, that for some proportions of replaced cells within a particular range there would be no answer to the question whether I was the same or a different person. Hence the indeterminacy and, too, Parfit's claim that an answer one way or the other would in any case be merely descriptive.

Now, a quick way in which to disarm this argument would be to make the case for its always being me, even when all my cells are replaced, and this clearly is correct from the first-person standpoint. That is, I wake up in the recovery room and immediately I am self-aware, the self in question being me, and without my having to check that it is by asking how much of my body has been replaced—for it makes no difference. Parfit would disagree; indeed, he is of the view that 'since the resulting person would be exactly like me, he would be inclined to believe that he was me. And this could not show that he *was* me, since any mere Replica of me would think that too' (p.299). What are we to make of this that could make any sense? Parfit seems to have conjured up two possible people, namely "he" and "me"; but I have just explained that I wake up after the operation and that my self is instantly in attendance, my self being me.

Can there be a replica of me who believes that he is me? Only if it were possible to fill in the details by which one may conceive of such a thing. Making the attempt, suppose I have an identical twin who answers to my name and claims to have written a philosophy book. But when he and I are in the same room, we both agree that we are distinct individuals with our own identities. Clearly, he does not really think that he is me, for how could he? Very well, then let there be one individual, not two, this being the case when my entire body is replaced. But I wake up and immediately am self-aware. Even if it were conceivable that I have been superseded by a replica of myself, what reason would there be for believing it? During the operation parts of me were replaced—in fact the whole of me. But I did not die on the operating table; indeed, I made a full recovery and here I am. Finally, we should keep in mind that such an operation is itself barely conceivable, not to mention inconceivable if one tries to flesh out the details. Are my cells replaced one by one? What a lengthy operation that would be! Parfit specifies that they would be replaced simultaneously; but what a conjuring trick that would be!

## 9.1: The Unimportance of Identity

What does Parfit mean when he seeks to show that personal identity is unimportant? In the second part of the chapter he develops this thesis in some detail. What counts, he says, is the psychological continuity and connectedness that personal identity consists in; it is in relation to these that the question of personal identity is unimportant, concerning as it does a merely linguistic fact. Moreover, such continuity is a matter of degree. I have tried to show that there are inconsistencies here, this being part of my wider aim of demolishing the framework within which Parfit's unimportance thesis is constructed. If I have succeeded, then the variable cell replacement argument turns out to be unsound, as does the claim that personal identity is distinct from the continuity it consists in. Set against Parfit's treatment of the issues involved is the view to which I have occasionally drawn attention: that personal identity does not consist in the continuity in question. For we can always ask what it is that unites particular experiences in relation to a particular individual, the answer to which is that he is the subject of such experiences, and in a way that seems to presuppose personal identity.

I say "seems" because whether it does or does not is a contentious question, as became apparent at the beginning of this chapter when we quoted from Ayer and Strawson. For Parfit the answer is that it does not, except that he then makes illicit use of the notion of distinct identity. It will be my contention that the concept of personal identity is irreducible within a system, with references to oneself and others being susceptible of analysis as avowals, this being far removed from Parfit's approach. Going deeper, and insofar as continuity involves the intentional, I shall maintain that the difficulty of the above question, and in general of issues of personal identity, derives from intentionality having its roots hidden in the non-conscious, about which nothing is known except that the nature of consciousness obliges us to postulate its existence. That said, and without such an appeal to the metaphysical, many theorists since the time of Descartes have not been deterred from forming an opinion, sometimes in favour of the Cartesian Ego that Parfit rejects, his preference being for a truly bizarre theory: one to which we now return.

Its essence is that if my replica on Mars can expect another forty years of life, then my imminent death here on Earth should matter very little to me. What matters, he says, is psychological connectedness and continuity, which he takes to obtain in the case of teletransportation. On that assumption, he says, 'I should regard this way of dying as being about as good as ordinary survival'. (p.215). Firstly, Parfit asks us to suppose that the replica and I are two distinct individuals, which clearly is correct, just as it would be with identical twins. It makes no difference if the replica calls himself by my name and claims to remember entering the machine and being told that his body will remain intact. Nothing alters the fact that there are two of us and that we cannot be the same person. When I die I will be dead, my replica still alive, perhaps for another forty years. This possibility is far more annoying than consolatory, its invidiousness difficult to account for if Parfit is correct, which in any case he cannot be.

His main argument is that myself on Earth and my replica on Mars are linked by psychological continuity and connectedness such that our recollections are the same, and, too, our abilities, for instance if I am writing a book. In that case, according to Parfit, if I die before the book is finished my replica will be able to finish it in just the way that I would. What he overlooks is that my future behaviour takes the form of interactions with my surroundings, which will be distinct for my replica from what they are for me. In any case, writing is creative and there is no reason to believe that my replica would finish the book in exactly the way that I would. One might as well expect identical twins to be exactly the same in every way, this being an extreme form of determinism. Note that

Parfit seems to have sidelined the bodily continuity criterion in favour of psychological continuity and connectedness as the pillar by which the unimportance thesis is elevated; but what is it about them that enables them to bear the weight? Keep in mind, given the implausibility of the thesis, that the pillar has to resist the lateral force, as it were, of the countervailing view, which is that the replica and I are separate and independent in the same way as any two people, in which case the thesis should be rejected.

What sets the replica and myself apart is that he is my clone, so that, for instance, his memory, or his library of memories, is the same as mine, as is his character, his personality and his genetic make-up. But these latter are no more relevant than they would be in the case of identical twins. To see this, let it be supposed that I do indeed have such a twin. Then although we may have a great deal in common, both genetically and as regards character and personality, neither of us is thereby more sanguine about dying, as if the survival of the other somehow compensates for death. If Parfit is correct, should we not breathe at least one sigh of relief, even if it is our last breath, at being survived by our twin?

## 9.2: The Unmaking of Assumptions

What, though, of the replica and I having the same memories? But the notion of shared recollections, if that is what they are, should not go unscrutinised—and neither should the idea of a replica. This is to say that we are now at the stage, as promised earlier, whereby we critically examine the notions involved and the assumptions that Parfit makes.

We are told that a machine on Earth prepares a blueprint of me and sends it to Mars, where another machine uses the blueprint to make my replica. But this is not even science fiction: rather, it is counter-scientific fantasy, with only very tenuous links to the restrictions that the real imposes on the possible. If we wish to be fully accountable to the world as it is, then we need to resist the rhetoric by which Parfit seeks to convert us to his quasi-immortalism. We gain immunity by not permitting him to beg the main questions, the secret of which, as Williams would say, inheres in his presentation.

Thus constrained, the following is what Parfit is entitled to say. First, that I enter a machine in a laboratory on Earth and a tangle of electrodes is attached to my head. Second, Alex tells me that a blueprint of me has been sent to, as it were, a twin laboratory on Mars. Third, he announces that the experiment has been a success, a replica of me having been created, and that it is in full working order. Smiling, I say 'Of course it is', and then I make my excuses and exit the building.

The next day, I am invited back and told that the replica, teletransported to Earth only an hour ago, is in the next room and eager to meet me. Thinking that the joke has gone too far, I shake hands with a man who could easily pass as my identical twin, except that each of us introduces himself as Laurence Peddle, whereas identical twins have different first names. Accusing him of being an impostor, I am taken aback when he denies the charge, in support of which he recounts in the first-person the birthday party at which Laurence piled his plate high with his favourite homemade cakes—those that are near enough for him to be able to grab them before anyone else can—and scoffed the lot.

Amazed, I ask myself how he could possibly know that they are the ones I like best, but we, looking on, do not need an answer, the argument already won. For it is very clear that this man and I are separate individuals, regardless of the prospects, even theoretically, for teletransportation. If, nevertheless, one insists that the existence of this replica, so-called, takes the sting out of my being mortal, then that really is a joke, and one that has gone far too far, the horses of the Apocalypse easily spooked.

Turning to memory, the main point has already been made: that memory presupposes personal identity. For present purposes this more than suffices, but sometimes too much is not enough, in which case we should ask what might be meant, exactly, by memory transfer, the new aim being to undermine the whole idea of shared recollection. Suppose that a mad scientist is let loose, anxious as she is to transfer another person's memories, say my identical twin's, into my head. When I awake from the operation, or when a magic wand is waved, the scientist is pleased with the way it all went. Fully recovered, I seem to remember a childhood party to which I was not invited, unlike my twin brother who by all accounts ate all the cakes. 'What an insecure child!' I exclaim, whereupon a friend who was also at the party all those years ago corrects me. 'You were at the party', he insists; 'it was your brother who was not invited. That was because children are easily confused. As for myself, I grew up with you both, and I could tell you apart. Besides, it was always you who scoffed all the cakes.'

What might I reasonably deduce from this? Only that it is all too common for an adult to mis-remember a childhood event. The appeal to recollective incorrectness would always triumph over the bizarre claim by a mad scientist as to intercranial memory transfer. Put another way, nothing would count as migration of that kind. Finally, it is not as if memory is distinct from other mental functions. On the contrary, it integrates with them within a system, so that it should be easy to show that where memory goes the mind goes with it, or would do if any of it made the slightest sense. That, however, would take up too much space.

If we now move on, we know that Parfit places emphasis on psychological continuity and connectedness as criteria of personal identity. He would say that since these are satisfied in the case of the replica, the question of personal identity lapses, or is only descriptive, or is of linguistic interest only. This is mad, our mission being to expose the madness.

In this we are making progress, the next step being to actually scrutinise the notions of psychological continuity and connectedness which according to Parfit link my earthly self with my Martian replica via the workings of the teletransportation system. But in what, exactly, or even very vaguely, do these notions consist? It has already been established that physical continuity is not a prerequisite of personal identity; hence my looking at a stranger in the mirror at the same time as I know that it is me. As for continuity of the psychological kind, it cannot refer to continuously being conscious, or not if one manages even the shortest nap. Is it, then, stability of personality and character? But one could never pin it down if that is the form by which we know it; and at what level, in any case, would the link to personal identity become apparent?

The upshot is that there is no reason, not in the slightest, why I should fear my imminent death less than I otherwise would, knowing as I do that an individual referred to as my replica, or less fantastically as my twin brother, may survive me by several years. And how could I possibly believe that my death will be almost as "good" as my own survival for that length of time? On the contrary, there will be a difference the enormity of which is enough to conjure up the elephant in the room; namely, that this individual will be alive and I will be *dead*.

## 9.3: Recapitulation and a Personal Identity Puzzle

In what does the concept of personal identity consist? According to Swinburne, unlike Parfit, this is not the same as asking about criteria. I have tried to show that Swinburne is correct in the distinction that he makes, but also that another distinction that between first- and third- person standpoints, following Williams, is equally important. If the concept of personal identity is irreducible, then a question arises as to the role of criteria. For Parfit, as we have seen, personal identity consists in psychological continuity and connectedness, a definition that we had occasion to reject. Also overboard went the bizarre theory, as I called it, about my death being, if not exactly therapeutic, at least at some level a good thing, provided that my replica replaces me on the bridge.

I tried to expose the flimsiness of the argumentative sails in support of this theory, to which end I advanced counter-arguments in favour of my own views on the nature of identity of this kind. Having outlined those views, I now propose to test them against one of Parfit's more extreme thought-experiments. Wishing to show again that identity is not what matters, Parfit assumes for that purpose the validity of the brain-based psychological criterion, as he calls it, such that the mind is causally dependent on the brain and goes where it goes. If my brain is transplanted into another body that is the body I wake up in after the operation. He also supposes that if the two hemispheres of my brain are separated, each will function in the same way as the intact brain.

Imagine, he says, that they are indeed separated, one of them transplanted into the empty head of another individual, the other preserved for future use. Then the person thus created is me, the same as before the operation. Going on the offensive, we claim that Parfit has already made unwarranted assumptions, taking for granted as he does that the brain recipient is me. Unwarranted, that is, because we are faced with fantasy, whereas the reality is that nothing is known about the personal identity outcome of such an operation, a fact concealed by Parfit's use of the first person. He is entitled to say only that one may imagine a surgeon performing a brain transplant from a subject to another individual's brainless body, a question then arising as to its outcome. Would the postoperative patient claim to be the subject? What we know is that he would be blessed with a sense of self, the same as any other individual. It is true that if the brain-based psychological criterion is assumed, then the identity obtains; but since we do not know that it does, we should not make that assumption.

Parfit is able to get away with assassinating reason, the surgeon perhaps guilty of actual murder or manslaughter, only because he smuggles empirical and conceptual assumptions into his account. Having escaped scrutiny, they give rise to a sense of intellectual unease that is difficult to trace back to them. That is why it is important to make the hidden connection, which I trust that we have succeeded in doing. What this means in the present case is that from the individual receiving the subject's brain it follows not at all that he is, or thinks he is, the subject. What does follow, this being the value of the exercise, is that it is conceivable that a person may wake up in a different body and with his personal identity intact. Or, on the other hand, that it remains intact even if his body changes out of all recognition. This is arguable because our bodies are indeed subject to severe change, albeit usually over a lifetime, not overnight.

Parfit now asks us to imagine that the preserved hemisphere is transplanted into a second body, the same as with the first, the two individuals being known as Mr A and Mr B. We should now agree, he says, that they cannot both be me, and by symmetry neither is a more suitable candidate than the other for that role, so neither of them is me. That is what Parfit says, but it seems to me that his use of the personal pronoun in this way is again tendentious, a point to which we shall return in a moment.

What, before then, should we say? We know what Parfit would say, and indeed he does not disappoint, arguing as he does that if they cannot be me (The personal pronoun again.) then personal identity is unimportant. What matters, he says, is that Messrs A and B satisfy the criterion; and yet, it is also Parfit's contention that if personal identity consists in brain-based psychological continuity and if that criterion is fulfilled, as in the case of Mr A and Mr B, then a further question as to whether personal identity obtains is merely verbal or descriptive. But he treats it as a substantive question when he states that if only Mr A has a brain hemisphere, the other in storage, then he and I are the same person, whereas if Mr B is given that other hemisphere, then I cannot be both of them and there is no reason to think that I am either of them. My existing if the one eventuality obtains but not if the other does is not a trivial result, a fact which indicates that Parfit equivocates in his use of the concept of personal identity.

How, then, should the analysis proceed? Firstly, we now have an additional reason to reject the brain-based criterion; namely, that it incurs the penalty of paradox in the form of A and B both having to be the donor, as against our contention that we do not or would not know what the personal identity connection would be. What we do know is that each of them has his own personal identity and sense of self. In so saying, we bear in mind that the very idea of a brain transplant is fantastical. Even so, is it not the case that the mental is causally dependent on the cerebral? No doubt it is, but the reference here is to empirical facts about correlations, whereas our concerns are philosophical.

Chief among these is the question of the link between criteria and personal identity, given that it cannot be by way of definitive feature or constitutive essence; as also, too, that the criteria at issue do not cope well with criticism, in particular from a first-person perspective. Using that advantage we have rejected criteria that appeal to memory, to bodily or psychological continuity, to physical resemblance or to brain states. Startled by a stranger when I look in the bathroom mirror, I am shocked to discover how much I have changed overnight. Conceivably, I now remember that yesterday my healthy brain in a moribund body was transplanted into the head of a fit and healthy younger man.

The difference between this and the cases we have critiqued is that we refer to what is conceivable, whereas Parfit takes the personal identity transfer to be entailed by the brain transplant. It is indeed entailed, but only if presupposed in the brain-based psychological criterion. That makes it emptily analytic, in connection with which it has been shown that the link between brain and mind is in fact a matter of empirical correlation.

If this is correct, then the conceivable is what counts, this being a fertile field in which to continue our transplant story, initially in the first-person. Suppose, slightly retrospectively, that I wake up after the operation, a place at the breakfast table of consciousness having been set for me, so that I immediately help myself to the self-awareness that is my prerogative as a member of the human race. Conceivably, I do not ask myself who I am; rather, I express that identity in one way or another. Perhaps I say to myself 'I'm not sure I did the right thing in having the operation. I feel about sixteen, which in fact is the age of this new body of mine. I'm thrilled to be young again, but what about the fact that the day before yesterday I was in my seventies? How will my partner react when she returns from her foreign holiday?' Or, there again, I wake up fully self-aware but the body of the past is empty of me, so that I shall have to learn how I once inhabited it. Or, I wake up as before and take today to be the first day of my life. Or none of the above.

Now consider the first possibility from a third-person perspective. Worried about his partner's reaction, Laurence asks his friend, Christopher, to vouch for him when she returns. But Christopher himself is taken aback when faced with a teenager who claims to be a septuagenarian. Again a protracted interrogation session ensues, with questions being asked about past shared experiences which Laurence, if it really is he, should be able to remember. These concern Cardiff University, broken spectacles, Gregynog Hall conferences, clubbing, dancing, writing, publishing and drones. Finally, Christopher contacts the surgeon who, it is claimed, performed the operation. Note that even with all answers correct and the surgeon's confirmation, Christopher is not obliged to accept the account on offer. It may seem to him that Laurence died on the operating table and thereby became an accidental brain donor, the recipient being a brainless teenager hitherto idling on a life support machine. Such divergencies of opinion, if taken to be the norm, are possible not in reality but in the fantasy world of the present case.

In recent paragraphs I have taken a dim view of Parfit's approach to personal identity criteria, which he insists on conflating with essential features of that identity. Such criteria, I maintained, presuppose personal identity; hence the ease with which they may be circumvented in particular cases. Waking up with complete recollection loss after an accident, one looks in a mirror and stares at the stranger who stares back. But neither amnesia nor bodily change impairs one's personal identity. Such criteria, in any case, are poorly aligned with personal identity and its uses.

There are, on the other hand, necessary conditions of discourse about the self, in particular in relation to the ascription of mental items to oneself and others within a sub-system. If I can ascribe them to myself but not to others, then I turn into a psychological solipsist, the only conscious human being, a position the absurdity of which is its own counter-argument. This is where the discussion deepens, for the nature of a system or sub-system is such as to permit in particular what is forbidden in general.

I can say that when I woke up after an accident I was unable to recollect anything prior to it; and, too, that when I looked in a hospital ward mirror I was shocked to see a stranger looking shocked. Surreal as this may seem, it impairs not at all my sense of self; for it is I, this person who I am, who has lost those memories and finds his appearance changed out of all recognition. But now, the sub-system would become unwieldy or fail altogether if sudden corporeal transformation became wide-spread, with people increasingly unable to identify one another, or even their past selves. This, or so I now maintain, is the kernel of truth in the notion of bodily continuity and resemblance as a criterion of personal identity. And the same, or similar, in the case of memory loss.

## 9.4: Going Deeper and Drawing Conclusions

Why is the nature of personal identity so resistant to analysis? There are criteria by which individuals on different occasions may or may not be the same person; but Parfit obscures the issues by taking criteria, or the conditions by which they are satisfied, as being that which personal identity consists in. We have seen that even as definitions they are inadequate to that role, the suspicion arising that personal identify is presupposed in any criterial account of what it consists in. Its elusiveness lends itself to the view that it is irreducible, this being the stance that we took. What is it, though, for a concept to be irreducible? There are parallels here with attempting to analyse intentionality; indeed, this latter enters into the analysis of personal identity at all points, as does the notion of an avowal.

That being the case, the mysterious nature of personal identity derives from its roots in the non-conscious, but there are surface indications of this deeper unknowability. Writing these words, I focus on the nature of personal identity in my own case, but there is nothing, really, to focus on. I am aware of a conscious flow, but what it amounts to is just my writing "I am aware...", concentration on which reveals not at all the hidden meaning of this reference to self. I said at the beginning that I am introspectively aware of my identity, but that was only in rejoinder to those who claim to be unable to make the acquaintance of their personal selves, as if these latter have to be introspectible objects in order to exist.

The metaphysical problem of the nature of personal identity is just that of the nature of the non-conscious and is thereby irresolvable. I know who I am, at least from one conscious moment to the next; but only if you do not ask me who I am or what it is to know it. The approach taken in this book and in *Beyond Knowledge* is either profoundly revealing of the presence of a hidden realm of truth or it is the ultimate in sceptical solutions—or it is both.

## 9.5: My Own Personal Identity and Self

What is it about personal identity issues that makes philosophers uncomfortable in their skin? 'Which skin would that be?' Parfit might ask, thereby fully answering the question, for the very idea of sharing one's identity among several individuals is anathema to the common man. It is also quite mad, but I have tried to show that it is possible for reason to prevail. That said, there are thought-experiments that prove instructive, as in the case of an old person waking up in a young person's body, the conceivability of which is part of the point to be made. Memory, too, or its dispensability in particular cases, is also a source of enlightenment, as is a qualification if the point is to hold. Quite simply, there are no cases in which memory from one moment to the next may be permitted to lapse. This is too obvious for micro-analysis to be needed.

We have seen that the loss of one's recollections prior to a particular event, together with bodily change, are conceivable in particular cases, this latter not being much of a stretch. For we know that we look different now from when we were children, and our sense of self would not be threatened if a change of appearance happened overnight. I can testify to this on the basis of my own experience when I suffered a very rapid weight loss and recoiled from the monster of emaciation staring at me when I looked in the mirror. This will be more perspicuous if we distinguish between the sense of self, of being the same person from one occasion to another, and the sense one has of oneself as an individual human being with one's own persona, central to which is its being manifested to others in the way that one looks and behaves. I recoiled because I knew that it was myself I was looking at. And, harking back to the preface, I was desperate not to die. Is that, one wonders, a clue of some kind, the puzzle being that of how it is that theorists with a perfectly serviceable brain can entertain Parfit's immortalism? Is it their own fear of death that interposes itself between rationality and belief?

Be that as it may, it is worth considering. For if Parfit's views are seized upon as a lifeline for those who are desperate to escape the sinking ship, the captain still on the bridge but his replicas commanding the boats and rafts, then those who cling to life may set a course not only for the Parfit mother ship on the horizon between life and death but also for another separation of earth and sky: that from which we, too, have made some extraordinary claims. One of these is the conscious inadequacy thesis whereby the intentional cannot be analysed exclusively in terms of conscious processes, one reason for which is that consciousness, in a special sense, is momentary, by which I mean that any reasoning, for instance, goes beyond the conscious moment. If I say out loud that '0.63 + 3.6 = 4.23', then by the time I utter the conclusion the terms to be summed no longer exist. I say '4.23' but by the time I say '3' the rest of the decimal has followed suit.

But the "3" belongs to a sum, which derives its content from the addition of two other numbers, so in some sense the whole of the addition must be in my mind when I state the sum; but even the "3" drops out of existence in the very act of my saying it. Since the calculation I make overruns each conscious moment, it must exist in the non-conscious, the same being true of all conscious processes; therefore, the nature of the non-conscious is unknowable, where this includes what it is that personal identity consists in. The non-conscious, then, is a mysterious realm, the word "mystery" having strong connotations.

Is it the case that we are under their spell when we contemplate what it is for ourselves to abruptly switch off? However that may be, there is nothing in my treatment of personal identity that can offer any hope to those whom death and dying implacably hunt down, which is to say to all of us old enough to think that we understand. Better, perhaps, to reject my views in favour of Parfit's, or better again, or at least more honest and direct, to convert to religion or, if one already has, to go to church more often.

Is there anything else that we can say about personal identity? The following may be of interest. In a previous chapter I emphasised how much is at stake when the sceptic about other minds throws down the gauntlet. Suppose, I said, that two people next to each other are gazing at a uniformly blue wall; then it is conceivable that their visual experience of the wall is exactly the same, even with regard to their sense of self. It is not, I said, as if one's individual identity runs though one conscious experience like a name through a stick of rock. Even if one has a sense of individual identity, there is no reason why it should not be the same experience for the two observers of the wall. If this is correct, then I do not know if or how it impinges on the mystery of personal identity; but I do know that if I discover a replica of myself, I shall have no compunction in reporting him to the police for identity theft, perhaps followed by suing him for plagiarism if it transpires that he, too, is writing my book.

What if, nodding in sympathy, we ask whether I would feel the same if I believed in a life after death? Parfit in a quite peculiar way does believe it, or so he claims, but the hereafter for him would seem to consist in joining one of the Martian colonies. This may suit some people, who perhaps in their desperation fall victim to interplanetary human traffickers and are abandoned in a crater on the far side of the Moon. But it appeals not at all to me, for my idea of heaven is to remain here on Earth and continue to circulate among my pleasures: I get up between six and seven, have breakfast or try to, and go jogging if the last time was the day before yesterday. On my return, or after breakfast, I do some writing and then I go out into the garden and work on the wind spinner. Then back to here to continue writing; then out into the garden again, and so on until eight or nine at night when I watch TV. Other people—the more the better—can migrate to Mars if they wish, where no doubt officials from the interplanetary immigration service will be waiting to interview them.

According to Parfit and others one should not be afraid to die if certain conditions obtain, though they do concede that death has its drawbacks, all the more so if dancing is the Saturday night of all one's days on Earth. The settlers on Mars would have to forgo the thrill of it if, as would presumably be the case, that entire godforsaken planet remained devoid of dance venues. It is not just that I love my life on Earth and Earth itself but that my friends and family are here, and I could never abandon them, or disappear from their lives as if they did not matter, or not if I had a choice. But surely, it will be said, other people may not share that view, speaking as they do of not being afraid of death, which they claim they will face with equanimity when the time comes.

This resignation in the face of the inevitable is, or so it seems, belied by, for instance, their driving the right way down a motorway—in fact by all the health and safety precautions that they take; but also, by their concern for the welfare of their friends and family, whom they wish to keep out of harm's way. But still, it is open to them to argue that much as they enjoy the party and wish to prolong it into the early hours, it cannot continue indefinitely, the guests leaving one by one as time goes on. The trick, they say, is to thank one's host for all the enjoyment that one has had, and then to depart not with regret but in celebratory mood. The problem here, however, is that this is an insipid metaphor for the attitude one should take to having to die; for there is nothing to celebrate if the party continues after one has left. Better, in my opinion, if the party is such that all the guests leave at the same time.

If that were the case, so that no-one will survive me when I die, perhaps as a result of an asteroid slamming into Earth, then I suspect that the fact of my imminent death would not horrify me in the way that it actually does. For a more realistic metaphor, there being nothing to celebrate, we need to return to the party that never ends, or only in the sense that individual guests leave the festivities and are replaced by others. That is one of the horrors of dying and being dead: that life continues without you, as if you had never been. Now consider the following humanist rejoinder to this negative approach to one's own mortality. Since we are all going to die, albeit not *en masse*, other things being equal, we should accept that fact and make the most of the time that remains to us. It is not, after all, as if we are going to miss being alive, for when we are dead we cease to miss anything.

That is the argument, or humanist argument, that many of us will be familiar with; but it seems to me to have not much life in it, or even to be moribund, for it is contradicted by such facts as that we find it rational and normal to feel deprived in advance if we have to miss out on, say, a forthcoming party that we are too ill to attend. Similarly, I feel sick with dread when I contemplate my missing out, posthumously, on all that makes me glad to be alive, where this includes not just the good but also the bad. I try to imagine my inexpressible joy if I were to be told that my cancer will always be with me but that I can expect to live another ten years.

None of this is to deny that some people may genuinely be accepting of their own mortality; but sometimes I am reminded of the behaviour of a zebra on the African plains when attacked by a lion. At first it fights back, the lion clinging to its neck, but at some point it ceases to struggle, the lion tightening its grip on its victim's throat. We pretend that there is no lion, or we imply it in the lies that we tell one another when we circle the wagons and conspire to self-deceive. 'We shall die with dignity', we chant in unison and shout into the gathering gloom, a child crying in the space thus created; and we other children at the dead centre of a void of nothingness that otherwise has no shape. Our words are met by silence, outlived not even by an echo—until, that is, the lions begin to roar as the night closes in. And then there is the bigger lie: that heaven awaits us; but the truth is that the hereafter is a dreadful place, or it would be if it existed.

For just suppose that shortly after you die, you find yourself looking at a screen and becoming aware of what it is that you are seeing. It is, in my case, your partner, and you watch her go from one room to another like a ghost, and you realise that she is looking for you, and as she weeps and calls out your name you are desperate to live again and go home, and to wait in your study for the door to open and this time for her to find you there. It was only a nightmare, you say, and perhaps at some future time that is all that it will be; but too late for us, and for our children's children. As things are, the door will open onto a malign emptiness, and a dreadful silence pervade the house, the garden and the shed.

## 9.6: Death and Mystery

If every human being alive today will die, and if there is no hereafter, or even if there is, then one must always ask whether it is possible to settle people's minds about the fate that awaits them. Is there any chance at all of administering the concept of mystery, as used in these pages, in order to deaden the pain? Even the non-reader may be struck by the difficulty, perhaps metaphysical in character, of imagining one's own death—or, rather, of grasping what it must be like to no longer be alive. The incoherence is plain to see, for nothing counts as the experience of being dead. But still we continue to gnaw at it, like rats through the side of a stricken ship.

Surely, though, it should be possible to lower the life raft of mysterianism into an angry sea, rather than to impotently rage, rage against the dying of the light.[8] In *Beyond Knowledge* I argue that radical solipsism—the theory that one is the only conscious human being—entails immortality; but only in the form of everlasting loneliness.

Stepping back from the deck rails, what of the hidden realm of the intentional? In *Beyond Knowledge* I contend that if the intentional resides not in the phenomenal but in the non-conscious, then in the sense of its being hidden we do not know what we mean. This includes reference to the past or to ourselves or other people. Since in a perfectly ordinary sense we do know what we mean, how are we to characterise the sense in which we do not, and in such a way as to turn the nightmare of death into just another dream? For the life of me, I cannot think how this might be achieved.

## 9.7: Last Words

Since these are the closing paragraphs of this book, I have been contemplating how most fittingly to fill them, given that the final pages of my biography are also being filled, albeit in invisible ink or visibly but in most parts illegibly, such is the uncertainty of it all. My consultant has, however, advised me not to make long-term plans, or perhaps just plans, and I noticed that the two paramedics in the corridor outside his room when I went in were still there when I left, whereupon they proceeded to follow me. As an act of defiance, I have sometimes made a point of writing fairly long sentences, and no doubt there will be others if time permits. During my deliberations it occurred to me that there was mileage to be had from a comparison between the endings of the last chapters of both volumes—that of *Beyond Knowledge* and this present chapter. Connecting their batteries, I managed to achieve ignition and now take off in first gear as follows.

The last chapter of *Beyond Knowledge*, on the meaning and the mystery of life, ended quite splendidly, I thought, and gained in lyricism what it lacked in Christian piety, Passages of purple prose, if one is a humanist, have their own temptations as the colour deepens, at least if the picture painted is that of Earth as potentially its own heaven. I did not, however, feel any urge to proselytise on behalf of humanism. That said, there was a kind of apotheosis, not of the abstractly spiritual but much more personally of accidental voluptuaries in the form of a young couple who chanced upon a mountain pool on a perfect summer day. The thrill of the cold on the heat of their sun-gilded skin, I wrote, was the ultimate fusion of the aesthetic and the sensual. Even in extremis, decades after the event, I see us reflected, the images merging as the bed of the stream gave us grip; and then the ripples deepening into waves of sensation; and the water slapping against the banks, flesh upon flesh; and in the ensuing quiet a celebratory skylark against such clarity of blue; and its purity of song so uplifting.

But the skylarks were losing altitude each summer, and the meadow pipits, too, went into a stall, and even the sparrows and starlings, the insects going then gone, including the meadow brown butterflies originally in their thousands, the famine emptying a chemical sky. Then the desolate silence when the myriad grasshoppers diminished to almost none, and the first year that the cuckoos never made it from Africa, or the elvers from the Sargasso Sea. Thus it is that much of nature became extinct in the valley, as elsewhere, and so it is that I am desperate not to die. My over-arching objective, while still alive and kicking into the void, is to finish this book and have it published, and soon thereafter to re-read it and quietly close it, the message in a bottle on its way to the sea. From the stream in the hills above Nantymoel to the Bristol Channel and beyond, an uncertain future will make its unpredictable move, and certainly I will never know how this human story ends....

## Inarticulate Grief

Let the sea beat its thin torn hands
In anguish against the shore,
Let it moan
Between headland and cliff;
Let the sea shriek out its agony
Across waste sands and marshes,
And clutch great ships,
Tearing them plate from steel plate
In reckless anger;
Let it break the white bulwarks
Of harbour and city;
Let it sob and scream and laugh
In a sharp fury,
With white salt tears
Wet on its writhen face;
Ah! let the sea still be mad
And crash in madness among the shaking rocks—
For the sea is the cry of our sorrow.

Richard Aldington

# Bibliography

Ashley, L. and Stack, M. (1974). 'Hume's Theory of the Self and its Identity' in Dialogue 13 (2): 239-254
Ayer, A. J. 1959. *Philosophical Essays* (London: Macmillan)
——1972. *Probability and Evidence* (London and Basingstoke: Macmillan)
——1973. *The Concept of a Person* (London and Basingstoke: Macmillan)
——1973a. *The Central Questions of Philosophy* (London: Weidenfield and Nicolson)
——1985. *Wittgenstein* (London: Weidenfield and Nicolson)
Barker, S. F. and Peter Achestein. Oct. 1960. 'On the New Riddle of Induction' in The Philosophical Review, Vol. 69
Bar-On, Dorit and Douglas C. Long. March 2001. 'Avowals and First-Person Privilege' in Philosophy and Phenomenological Research, Vol. 62
Bellos, Alex. 2016. *Can You Solve My Problems?* (London: Guardian Books)
Blackburn, Simon. 1973. *Reason and Prediction* (London: Cambridge University Press)
Baker, G. P. and P. M. S. Hacker. 1984. *Scepticism, Rules and Language* (Oxford: Basil Blackwell)
——1985. *Wittgenstein: Rules, Grammar and Necessity* (Oxford: Basil Blackwell)
Carnap, Rudolph. 2013. *The Unity of Science* (Routledge)
Cassam, Quassim. 2007. *The Possibility of Knowledge* (Oxford University Press)
Chalmers, David J. 1995. 'Facing up to the Problem of Consciousness' in Journal of Consciousness Studies, No. 3
Dainton, Barry. 2005. 'The Self and the Phenomenal' in *The Self?* (Blackwell Publishing Ltd)
DeRose, Keith. 1999. 'Solving the Sceptical Problem', in *Scepticism: A Contemporary Reader*, ed. by DeRose, Keith and Ted A. Warfield (Oxford: Oxford University Press)
Dretske, Fred. 1999. 'Epistemic Operators', in *Scepticism*, ed. by DeRose and Warfield

Fisher, Ronald A. 1947. *The Design of Experiments* (Edinburgh: Oliver& Boyd)
──1956. *Statistical Methods and Scientific Inference* (Edinburgh: Oliver& Boyd)
Gelman, Andrew. 2008. 'Objections to Bayesian Statistics', in Bayesian Analysis
Gelman, Andrew and C. P. Robert. 2013. 'Not Only Defended But Also Applied: The Perceived Absurdity of Bayesian Inference' in The American Statistician, Vol.67
Goodman, Nelson. 1983. *Fact, Fiction and Forecast* (Harvard University Press)
Grayling, A. C. 2008. *Scepticism and the Possibility of Knowledge* (London; New York: Continuum)
Grice, H. P. 1957. 'Meaning', in Philosophical Review
Harrod, R. 1974. *Foundations of Inductive Logic* (Macmillan)
Hattiangadi, Anandi. 2007. *Oughts and Thoughts* (Oxford; Oxford University Press)
Howson, Colin. 2000. *Hume's Problem* (Oxford; Clarendon Press)
Hume, David. 1975. *An Enquiry concerning Human Understanding*, ed. Nidditch (Oxford University Press)
──2003. *A Treatise of Human Nature*, edited and abridged by Wright, John P, Robert Stecker and Gary Fuller (London; Everyman)
Huxley, Aldous. 1972. *The Doors of Perception* (Chatto & Windus)
Jackson, Frank. March 1975. 'Grue' in The Journal of Philosophy, Vol. 72
James, William. 1950. *The Principles of Psychology* (Dover Publications)
Jones, O. R. ed. 1971. *The Private Language Argument* (Toronto; Macmillan)
Keynes, J. M. 1973. *A Treatise On Probability* (London and Basingstoke: Macmillan)
Kripke, Saul A. 1982. *Wittgenstein on Rules and Private Language* (Oxford: Basil Blackwell)
Kuhn, T. S. 2012. *The Structure of Scientific Revolutions* (University of Chicago Press)

Lange, Mark. 2002. 'Okasha On Inductive Scepticism' in The Philosophical Quarterly, Vol.52.
Law, Stephen. 2004. 'Five Private Language Arguments', in International Journal of Philosophical Studies 12, No.2
Locke, John. 1997. *An Essay Concerning Human Understanding* (Penguin Classics)
Macdonald, Cynthia. 1998. 'Externalism and Authoritative Self-Knowledge' in *Knowing Our Own Minds* (Oxford: Oxford University Press)
Madell, Geoffrey. 1976. 'Ayer on Personal Identity' in Philosophy, Vol. 51, No. 195, pp 47-55
Martin, C. B. and J. Heil. 1998. 'Rules and Powers' in Philosophical Perspectives, Vol. 12, Language, Mind and Ontology, 283-312
McDowell, John. 1998. *Mind, Value and Reality* (Cambridge, Mass.: Harvard University Press)
—— 1998. 'Response to Crispin Wright' in Smith, B. C, and C. Wright and C. Macdonald eds. *Knowing Our Own Minds* (Oxford: Oxford University Press)
McGinn, Colin. 1984. 'What is the Problem of Other Minds?' Proceedings of the Aristotelian Society, Supplementary Volume 58, pp. 119-137.
——1987. *Wittgenstein on Meaning* (Oxford: Basil Blackwell)
——1991. *The Problem of Consciousness* (Cambridge Mass.: Blackwell)
McGinn, Marie. 2007. *Routledge Philosophy Guidebook to Wittgenstein and the Philosophical Investigations* (United Kingdom: Taylor and Francis Ltd)
Mellor, D. H. 2004. *Probability: A Philosophical Introduction* (Routledge)
Miller, Alexander 1998. *Philosophy of Language* (London: UCL Press)
Moore, G. E. 1959. *Philosophical Papers* (New York: Collier Books)
Nickerson, R. S. 2004. *Cognition and Chance: The Psychology of Probabilistic Reasoning* (Psychology Press)
Nagel, Thomas. 1979. *Mortal Questions* (Cambridge: Cambridge University Press)

Ogden, Charles K. and I. A. Richards. 1989. *The Meaning of Meaning* (Mariner Books)

Okasha, Samir. 2001. 'What Did Hume Really Show About Induction?' The Philosophical Quarterly, Vol. 51. No. 204.

Parfit, Derek. 1984. *Reasons And Persons* (New York: Oxford University Press)

Peacocke, Christopher and Colin McGinn. 1984. 'Consciousness and Other Minds', in Proceedings of the Aristotelian Society, Supplementary Volumes, vol. 58, 97–137.

Pears, David. 1988. *The False Prison: A Study of the Development of Wittgenstein's Philosophy* (Oxford: Oxford University Press)

Peddle, Laurence. 2021. *The Mystery Beyond Knowledge:Scepticism, Intentionality, and the Non-Conscious* (Cambria Publishing)

——2022. *Self, System, and the Non-Conscious: The Further Metaphysics of Meaning and Mystery* (Cambria Publishing)

Penelhum, Terence. 1971. 'The Importance of Self-Identity' in The Journal of Philosophy,Vol. 68, no. 20.

Quine, W. V. O. 1953. *From a Logical Point of View* (Cambridge, Mass.: Harvard University Press)

Russell, Bertrand. 1995. *Portraits From Memory* (Spokesman Books)

Shoemaker, Sydney. June 1994. 'Self Knowledge and "Inner Sense"' in Philosophy and Phenomenological Research, Vol. 54

Smith, A. D. 2002. *The Problem of Perception* (Cambridge: Harvard University Press)

Smith, Barry C. 1998. 'On Knowing One's Own Language' in *Knowing Our Own Minds* (Oxford: Oxford University Press)

Steup, M. and E. Sosa. 2005. *Contemporary Debates in Epistemology* (Blackwell Publishing Ltd)

Stern, Robert. 2000. *Transcendental Arguments and Scepticism* (New York: Oxford University Press)

Stone, James V. 2013. *Bayes Rule: A Tutorial Introduction to Bayesian Analysis* (Sebtel Press)

Stove, D. C. 1986. *The Rationality of Induction*
    (Oxford: Clarendon Press)
Strawson, Galen. 2009. *Selves: An Essay in Revisionary Metaphysics* (Oxford University Press)
Strawson, P. F. 1952. *Individuals: An Essay in Descriptive Metaphysics* (London: Methuen)
Stroud, Barry. 2004. *Meaning, Understanding, and Practice*
    (Oxford: Oxford University Press)
Swinburne, R. G. 1974. 'Personal Identity' in Proceedings of the Aristotelian Society, New Series, Vol. 74, pp 231-447
Tallis, Raymond. 2016. *Aping Mankind* (Routledge Classics)
    (Oxford: Oxford University Press)
Weatherford, Roy. 1982. *Philosophical Foundations of Probability Theory* (London: Routledge and Kegan Paul)
Williams, Bernard. 1970. 'The Self and the Future' in
    The Philosophical Review, Vol. 79, No. 2, pp. 161-180
Williams, D. C. 1947. *The Ground of Induction*
    (Cambridge, Mass.: Harvard University Press)
Williams, Michael. 1996. *Unnatural Doubts: Epistemological Realism and the Basis of Scepticism* (Princeton, New Jersey: Princeton University Press)
Wittgenstein, Ludwig. 1969. *On Certainty*
    (Oxford: Basil Blackwell)
——1976. *Philosophical Investigations*

# Endnotes

[1] In *Probability and Evidence* and in *Language, Truth and Logic*. See bibliography
[2] See Nickerson (2004) in the bibliography
[3] See Ayer's *Probability and Evidence*.
[4] Product rule: if events *a* and *b* are independent, then
$$P(a \cap b) = P(a) \times P(b).$$
[5] This recalls the account of the dynamics of competing scientific theories presented in Thomas Kuhn's *The Structure of Scientific Revolutions*.
[6] This notion of working in the dark is the one that binds together the different aspects of probability theory under discussion, but also it weaves in and out of all the chapters, its connections being very many. Wittgenstein refers to rules being followed blindly, but my present point about probability methods is that very little light can be shed on why they work or what counts as their being effective. Their success is judged, after all, by appeal to probability theory itself, as in the case of the link between poor quality research being published and allegedly lax levels of significance. The theory is essential to the judging of quality.
[7] It is worth noting that the notion of necessary conditions of concept application does have affinities with Wittgenstein, but very vaguely, if only for the reason that his utterances are so far underground. Given their warren-like depth, or perhaps obscurity, one has little idea which of the exits into communicable meaning they will take, the rabbits never out of the hat for long.

[8] Dylan Thomas- 1914-1953

## Do not go gentle into that good night

Do not go gentle into that good night,
Old age should burn and rave at close of day;
Rage, rage against the dying of the light.

Though wise men at their end know dark is right,
Because their words had forked no lightning they
Do not go gentle into that good night.

Good men, the last wave by, crying how bright
Their frail deeds might have danced in a green bay,
Rage, rage against the dying of the light.

Wild men who caught and sang the sun in flight,
And learn, too late, they grieved it on its way,
Do not go gentle into that good night.

Grave men, near death, who see with blinding sight
Blind eyes could blaze like meteors and be gay,
Rage, rage against the dying of the light.

And you, my father, there on the sad height,
Curse, bless, me now with your fierce tears, I pray.
Do not go gentle into that good night.
Rage, rage against the dying of the light.